"From his perspective of rich pastoral ministry, Peter Lord supplies great insight to life's biggest challenges. His pastoral guidance and sound scriptural perspective make this book a must-read for all disciples on their journey of growth and service to God."

Robert Morris, senior pastor, Gateway Church, Southlake, Texas; bestselling author of *The Blessed Life*, *From Dream to Destiny* and *The God I Never Knew*

"Have you ever dreamed of having your own personal coach to motivate and encourage you on your life's journey? *10 Secrets to Life's Biggest Challenges* will inspire you with insights and practical tips in overcoming ten major challenges everyone will inevitably face."

Johnny Hunt, senior pastor, First Baptist Church, Woodstock, Georgia; former president, Southern Baptist Convention

"Peter Lord's teachings have deeply impacted my life. God has gifted him with wisdom and the ability to apply God's Word to everyday life. This book is a fantastic resource to equip every believer with the knowledge and skills necessary to overcome in every circumstance."

Jimmy Evans, founder and CEO, Marriage Today

10
SECRETS
TO LIFE'S
BIGGEST
CHALLENGES

10

SECRETS
TO LIFE'S
BIGGEST
CHALLENGES

HOW YOU CAN PREPARE FOR A BETTER TOMORROW

PETER LORD

WITH KENT CROCKETT

Chosen

a division of Baker Publishing Group
Minneapolis, Minnesota

Published by Chosen Books
11400 Hampshire Avenue South
Bloomington, Minnesota 55438
www.chosenbooks.com

Chosen Books is a division of
Baker Publishing Group, Grand Rapids, Michigan

Printed in the United States of America

Library of Congress Cataloging-in-Publication Data is available for this title.

ISBN 978-0-8007-9539-9 (pbk.)

Cover design by Lookout Design, Inc.

12 13 14 15 16 17 18   7 6 5 4 3 2 1

To the many wonderful saints that I have known during my lifetime. To me they will always be Hebrews 11 saints—men and women of faith who made an impact on eternity. Thank you for being legitimate expressions of Jesus to many others and to me.

CONTENTS

FOREWORD

You will face many different challenges throughout your life. Trying to figure out how to solve every problem can be an overwhelming task, but suppose you could separate and group them under ten topics. In this book, Peter Lord addresses the ten biggest challenges in life and explains how to solve them.

This book will give you guidelines to help you make the right decisions. Peter analyzes how Adam and Eve were tempted and explains how the tactics Satan used in the Garden of Eden are still in operation today. He explains three important principles that make relationships work and the secrets of resolving conflict. If you have been hurt, you will discover how to forgive and let go.

I have known Peter Lord for many years. He has spoken at my conferences and has been a guest on my television program, *Life Today*. Peter is one of the most gifted Bible teachers that I have ever heard, and his insights into God's Word have liberated many people.

He is the bestselling author of *Hearing God*, and I am so glad that he wrote another book of advice to help people in this very troubled world. Peter's co-author, Kent Crockett, has added some of his own insights that he gained from being a pastor and counselor for over thirty years.

I hope that you will read this book and the information will become a reality in your life. God wants you to be a spiritual champion, but that can only happen if you use wisdom as you encounter each problem. So open your heart and allow God to teach you the ten secrets to life's biggest challenges.

James Robison
President, LIFE Outreach International
Fort Worth, Texas

ACKNOWLEDGMENTS

I would like to give special thanks to the following:

To my precious wife, Johnnie, for serving the Lord with me in ministry for all these years and being a living example of Jesus Christ.

To Wanda Rogers and David Hosely, for your insights that helped me write this book.

To James and Betty Robison, for your friendship. Your work with LIFE Outreach International is making an incredible impact in reaching people both in the United States and around the world.

To Jane Campbell, Natasha Sperling, Tim Peterson, Elisa Tally, Christina Files, and the entire team at Chosen Books for the wonderful work you do to further God's Kingdom.

INTRODUCTION

I am in the fourth quarter of the game of life and it will not be long before God calls me to the locker room. Before I go to my permanent home in the next life, I want to leave some advice for those who might be in the first or second quarter of their lives.

If you are at halftime (midlife), you might need to make some adjustments so you can play better in the second half. Since you do not know how long you will live, you might also be in your fourth quarter. No one knows when the game will end.

In this book I have listed the top ten challenges that you will face in life, and I will act as an assistant coach to help you become a better player. A coach cannot go out on the field to take a player's place. He or she can only show an athlete what to do in any given situation. I cannot play the game of life for you, but I can pass along some insights I have learned from my own experiences on the field.

One challenge that you will face involves making decisions. I cannot make your decisions for you, but I can coach you about how to make wise choices from God's playbook. Another tough opponent is temptation. You can win this battle once you understand a few key truths. I will also share some tips about resolving conflicts, managing your money, and maintaining a good attitude. The Lord is actually the Head Coach, and He can give you the wisdom and power to live victoriously in this game called life.

I have written this ten-lesson manual not only for your own personal growth, but also to be used in small groups and Sunday school classes. The questions at the end of each chapter will help to guide your discussion.

Before you read any further, I invite you to pray this prayer:

Heavenly Father, please fill me with the Holy Spirit right now. I ask You to enlighten me on the practical truths I need to know and to give me the power and motivation to carry them out. In Jesus' name, Amen.

Peter Lord

MAKING DECISIONS

Destiny is not a matter of chance. It is a matter of choice.
—William Jennings Bryan

When I was the pastor of Park Avenue Baptist Church in Titusville, Florida, I was praying one day in early December. Suddenly these words popped into my mind: *I want you to construct a building where people can pray. As proof that this is My idea and not yours, I will send someone to the church that you do not know who will give five hundred dollars toward the building.*

It was not an audible voice, but it came to me in my thoughts. I wrote in my prayer journal what the Lord had said. The next day I was praying about the chapel when more words came: *This will happen before Christmas.*

Again I recorded what God had told me, but I did not tell anyone. I did not want some well-meaning person to try to be the fulfillment.

Over two weeks passed, but no one brought me any money. I started to doubt what I had heard. Time was running out. I prayed, *Lord, are You sure You didn't mean by New Year's Day?* I thought I would give Him a little more time to perform the miracle!

Silence. No words came to my mind. Since He had told me "before Christmas," I guessed He must have meant what He had spoken the first time.

Then a few days before Christmas, a married couple from another city pulled into the church parking lot. They walked into the church and asked to speak to me. The church secretary buzzed my office. "Pastor, there is a couple here who wants to talk with you."

I invited the couple into my office, where they introduced themselves. They said, "Pastor, you don't know us, but God spoke to us when we were praying. He told us to come here and give you some money. We don't really understand why we needed to drive here to give this to you; we're just being obedient." The couple handed me a check for $500!

Not only did this couple give the first gift, but they later contributed an even larger amount. We constructed the prayer chapel, which many people have used to intercede for others.

The Lord guided me in making a decision by speaking words to my mind. He can do the same for you. Since you will be making thousands of choices throughout your lifetime, it is the first challenge we will tackle. Let us take a look at some of the principles involved in making a decision.

Principles of Decision-Making

Who is going to run your life? Is God calling the plays, or are you? How you answer these questions will determine how your life will turn out.

It all started at the beginning of Creation, when Adam and Eve were put in the Garden of Eden and God told them what they could and could not do. The Lord gave them permission to eat from any tree in the Garden, but He put a restriction on one tree that they could not eat from—the Tree of the Knowledge of Good and Evil (see Genesis 2:9). Although they had probably made a few minor decisions before this, they had never had to choose between good and evil. Their wrong choice brought sin into the world, and people have been choosing between good and evil ever since then. It is imperative that we understand the principles involved in making decisions. Once we grasp the ramifications of our choices, we will take them more seriously.

Principle #1: Every Decision Is an Exchange

Several years ago, a popular radio program called *Swap Shop* aired in our town. People could call in to the show and swap what they had for an item that another caller was offering. Some people made good trades, while others got burned.

Life is like a swap shop. Every decision is an exchange, where we give up one thing to get something else. We are constantly trading one thing for another. If you go to a furniture store, you hand cash to the salesperson and walk out of the store with a chair. You have made an exchange by giving up money in exchange for a piece of furniture.

When you exchange wedding vows, you make a decision to give up your single life for married life. You give up the right to keep dating others because you are committing yourself to one person for the rest of your life. If you decide to move to another city, you leave where you currently live to go to a new location. You are exchanging one place for another.

Everything you are willing to let go of has a price tag in your mind, as does the item that you want. To make a wise exchange, you must correctly determine the value of each. If you get it wrong on your evaluation, you are probably going to make a deal that you will end up regretting.

In the Old Testament, Esau made an incredibly dumb decision because he did not understand the value of what he had. When he came in from hunting one day, Jacob was cooking stew. Jacob offered him a bowl, but only if Esau would hand over his birthright to him. Esau was so hungry, he did not think through the consequences of his decision. He said, "Behold, I am about to die; so of what use then is the birthright to me?" (Genesis 25:32). He swapped his birthright, which was his inheritance, for a bowl of soup. He made an unbelievably foolish decision because the only thing on his mind was satisfying his immediate need.

So many people make choices just like Esau. They do not think through their decisions, or the value of what they have, so they give up something precious to satisfy their momentary urges. Later, they kick themselves for their decision. After Esau made the swap, he tried to get back what he had given up. Even though he sought it by crying, his heart never changed (see Hebrews 12:17).

The most important exchange you will ever make has eternal consequences. Jesus said, "For what profit is it to a man if he gains the whole world, and loses his own soul? Or what will a man give in exchange for his soul?" (Matthew 16:26, NKJV). The price tag Jesus put on the soul was more than all the wealth in the entire world. Who would have thought that your eternal soul, which is inside your body, is worth that much? The only way we know this is through His revelation. Whether you believe His words or not will determine what you do with your soul.

Many people do not realize the value of their souls because they cannot see them, and so they will exchange them for the pleasures of this life. One day they will find out they have made a bad trade, but by then it may be too late. Like Esau cried about his foolish decision, many others will weep over selling their souls for this life instead of living for the next life.

Principle #2: Every Decision Has a Consequence

Every decision has a consequence. Life is not a Monopoly game. You cannot put your money down, move a few pieces around, and walk away whenever you want. Life's choices are for keeps. When you make the right decisions, you will discover God's will for your life.

Just stop and think of how many choices you have already made today. By the end of the week you will have probably made hundreds of decisions. We make them so often that we have become desensitized to the consequences of our choices. The life you are now living is the result of all your past decisions.

Paul told us, "Do not be deceived, God is not mocked; for whatever a man sows, this he will also reap" (Galatians 6:7). When you sow an action, you will reap a consequence. You can choose the road you travel on, but you cannot choose where it leads. The destination is already set.

Keep this truth in mind whenever you make a decision. Over time, your actions have produced your current character, lifestyle and circumstances. Your life right now is a direct result of the choices you have made.

No blaming others for your problems. No finger pointing. Do not be like Adam, who told God after he had sinned, "The woman that *you* gave me caused me to do it." You must take responsibility for the decisions you make.

The bigger the decision you make, the greater the consequence. Major decisions usually involve a higher risk and a longer commitment. These would include such things as getting married, changing jobs, moving to a new location, or buying a house. Minor decisions can seem insignificant and unimportant at the moment, but many of them have long-term consequences. An acorn is very small, but given time, it will become an oak tree.

A counselor friend of mine told me about a man who was addicted to pornography. It began when he looked at a magazine he found lying on the ground while he was running. Just one look led to enslavement. That is why it is important to think about the outcome of your decision down the road and how it will affect you.

The bigger the decision you make, the greater the consequence.

If you have ever driven along the interstate in the South, you may have seen miles and miles of Kudzu vines covering trees and bushes along the highway. No one planted it there. It spread from somewhere else and is now out of control.

Kudzu was not native to America but was imported from Japan. Why would someone want to bring it here? It all started about 1935, when farmers were encouraged to plant it to reduce soil erosion during the Dust Bowl years. It looked like a great idea at first, but they did not think about the problems it would create in the future. Kudzu spreads so quickly that it becomes uncontrollable.

When making a decision, do not just look at how it immediately fixes your problem. Think down the road about how it will affect your future. Will the decision you are making become a long-term blessing, or will it become a Kudzu vine?

Too many people want instant gratification and ignore the disastrous consequences that are sure to come. Many people are in deep financial trouble because they keep charging items on their credit cards. They buy whatever they see, even if they do not really need it, and only consider if they can afford the minimum balance. They do not realize that the interest is compounding over time and is creating a crushing debt obligation.

Wise people make their decisions by thinking about long-term consequences. Foolish people make choices by only considering what will meet their immediate desires. Which are you?

CHOICES CAN HAVE UNINTENDED CONSEQUENCES

Many young people are willing to exchange their virginity for a moment of pleasure. They usually are not thinking about the unintended consequences, such as a sexually transmitted disease, a guilty conscience, an unwanted pregnancy, or regrets when they end up marrying someone else. Those who experiment with drugs never see the addiction coming. If they envision the inevitable consequences *before* they begin the decision-making process, it will keep them from making bad choices.

Unexpected consequences do not only apply to the bad decisions people make. Good choices can also have unplanned results, which are the serendipities of life.

Years ago, I developed a plan to help people in prayer. At first, it started as a small booklet to help people in my congregation. But God had some greater things in mind. People outside the church also wanted copies. Soon it was going to other states, and finally it was distributed to people all over the world. I never dreamed that 35 years later over 400,000 copies of *The 2959 Plan* would be printed.[1] Even as I write this, I got a request from Hawaii for more copies of the prayer plan. That seemingly small decision to write down

1. This book is available at www.PeterLord.net.

a plan turned into something much larger than I could ever have imagined.

Choices Can Also Have Intended Consequences

Wise people will make decisions in order to receive a planned result. Farmers will make a decision to plant seeds in a field because they want to produce a harvest. They understand the laws of the harvest: We reap *what* we sow, *later than* we sow, and *more than* we sow.

What is true in the agricultural kingdom is also true in God's Kingdom. Jesus told us to "lay up for yourselves treasure in heaven" (Matthew 6:20, NKJV). One way to do this is to give your tithes and offerings to Him with a cheerful heart. The question is, do you really believe what He said? Do you really believe that when you die, you will see the treasure that you have been laying up during your lifetime on earth?

Christians all over the world truly believe that what Jesus said is true, so they faithfully give their offerings for an intended consequence—to receive treasure in heaven after they die. They exchange money on earth for treasure in heaven. So is that a good trade? We will all find out after we die.

Principle #3: Every Decision Is Driven by a Motive

Have you ever asked yourself, *Why did I do that? Why didn't I do that? Why did I quit school?* What motivates your decisions? You can do the right thing with the wrong motive, or the wrong thing with the right motive. God says that one day He will disclose the motives of our hearts (see 1 Corinthians 4:5).

It would be wise to examine some of the reasons people make certain decisions on life's journey. If we understand the motives for decision-making, it can deter us from making bad choices and help us to make the right ones in the future.

As you look at the following reasons, I would like you to reflect on your own past decisions. Ask yourself if you have ever made a choice based on these motives:

NEEDS

A particular need might motivate a person to make a specific decision. You decide to eat because you are hungry. There is nothing wrong with that. But you also decide *what* you will eat. Once you put it in your mouth and swallow it, whatever you ate will affect you in a good or bad way. If you eat something nutritious, it will benefit your body. But you cannot have three helpings of chocolate cake and tell it to turn into muscle. You cannot eat something spoiled or rotten without getting sick.

PROFIT

The desire to gain a profit might motivate a person to make a specific decision. Most of the people who invest in the stock market want to make a profit. We make that choice because we believe we will benefit from it. This is not wrong, but we need to make a profit for the right reasons.

We need to be aware, however, of Pyrrhic victories. A Pyrrhic victory occurs when one wins the battle but loses the war. The term comes from history, when King Pyrrhus defeated the Romans at Heraclea in 280 B.C. Ironically, the enormous cost it took to win the battle also caused him to lose the war.

I read about a woman who was building a business so that her family would live the "dream life." But it took her so many hours away from her family, and created so much stress with her husband and kids, that all they could do was fight when they finally went on the dream cruise! She won the battle but lost the war. If your decision is to make a profit, make sure that it will not be at the cost of losing something more valuable. If everything checks out, then it is okay to proceed.

GREED

One of the detrimental mentalities of our society is the urge for instant gratification, where a person says, "I have to have it now!" Where does this idea come from?

Those who struggle with greed may have been raised in homes of luxury. It might have taken their parents thirty years to reach that level of income and to accumulate their possessions, but they were born into those surroundings. Luxury may be all they have ever known. They were not around when their parents started in poverty years before.

When children leave home and get married, they often want to instantly live at the same standard of living that they left. They want to buy a nice house and a fancy car, but they do not want to wait. They realize they can have it right now if they can borrow long-term and afford the minimum payments. Ultimately, this puts tremendous and unnecessary pressure on the marriage, which can create other problems as well.

EASIEST PATH

Many people will make their decisions by choosing the path of least resistance. When you are tired, or at a point of weakness, that is a dangerous time to make a decision. You will be attracted to the easiest way out instead of choosing the right path. Sometimes the correct choice is the most difficult road to travel. The quick, easy solution usually results in long-term pain and regret. Remember that the bitterness of poor quality lingers long after the sweetness of cheap price has been forgotten.

PEER PRESSURE

In this world, peer pressure is one of the strongest influences that can affect a person's decisions. Most people do not want their friends and colleagues to think badly about them, so they will sometimes compromise their principles in order to stay in favor with them. Generally speaking, young people are more worried about being popular than making correct choices. If the pressure from the outside is greater than the conviction on the inside, that person is going to cave in.

Although young people are most likely to please their peers, the desire to conform knows no age limit. In my retirement years, I have been greatly tempted to just take it easy for the rest of my life. This temptation is strengthened whenever I see people my age constantly going on cruises and living "the good life" of retirement.

> **If the pressure from the outside is greater than the conviction on the inside, that person is going to cave in.**

I believe that I am running a race and that race will not be over until I die. I have decided that I need to keep working in God's Kingdom, and so I still lead small group Bible studies, speak in churches and write my devotions.

To keep me motivated, I seek to hang around those who will encourage me to keep going. The Bible warns us, "Bad company corrupts good morals" (1 Corinthians 15:33). The opposite is also true. Good company prevents bad morals.

PLEASING GOD

The apostle Paul wrote that it is our ambition to be pleasing to the Lord (see 2 Corinthians 5:9). If our primary desire is to gain God's approval, we will make the right choices. The greatest command is to love God with all our hearts, and the second greatest commandment is to love our neighbor as ourselves. Spirit-filled Christians are motivated by God's love, which the Holy Spirit pours out in their hearts.

Although God wants us to love our neighbors, we should not seek to please others above our desire to please God. Some of the Pharisees believed in Jesus but would not talk about it because they were afraid of being ejected from the synagogue, "for they loved the approval of men rather than the approval of God" (John 12:43).

> **Even bad choices usually look good to us when we make them.**

Ultimately, we will give an account to God for the decisions we have made. "So then each one of us shall give an account of himself to God" (Romans 14:12). With this in mind, we must be especially careful how we make our decisions.

The Decision-Making Process

Some decisions are easy. Others are very difficult. Since every choice affects you for better or worse, it only makes good sense to have a process by which you will make your decisions. Sometimes you are forced into making choices, and although you might not want to decide, you must. A failure to make a decision is in itself a decision that has consequences.

Even bad choices usually look good to us when we make them. No one makes a wrong decision and then says, "I know I am making a stupid decision and the consequences are going to be disastrous, but I am okay with that." No one says this because, at that moment, the choice seems reasonable and good—and maybe even best. Bad decisions can be disguised and present themselves as the good answer we have been looking for.

Eve thought picking the forbidden fruit was a good decision. It looked delightful, not evil. She thought it would make her wise, not a fool. Eating the forbidden fruit seemed like a good decision while she was "under the influence."

Esau also thought his decision was a good one when he exchanged his birthright for a bowl of soup. Think of the number of people who bought stock in a company that looked good, only to find out things were not as they appeared to be.

I had the chance to buy stock in a company that was making biodiesel fuel from hamburger grease. They claimed to have a working plant that was supposedly doing this. At the time, it looked like everyone who bought stock was going to hit the jackpot. But now the people running the company are serving time in prison and the investors are poorer for it. Clearly, buying this stock looked like a great decision and a wonderful opportunity, but it turned out to be just the opposite.

> **A good decision is one that you never have to be sorry for.**

A good decision is one that you never have to be sorry for. The best evidence of a good choice is that you never regret the consequences of it. I have never regretted marrying my wife, or choosing the vocation that I have had for the last sixty years. After coming to the United States from Jamaica, I have not regretted becoming an American citizen. I made all of these decisions after much prayer, and the Lord pointed me down the right road.

Of course, you will also be in situations when others will make decisions for you. When you were young, your parents made important decisions for you. Whenever you place yourself under someone's authority, such as being hired for a job, they will make certain decisions that will affect you. In your elderly years, if your physical or mental abilities deteriorate, your children or others will make decisions for you.

Yet, even within these circumstances, you will still have choices to make involving your attitude and actions. Your happiness depends upon it. That is why Paul, who was confined to a Roman prison against his will, made a decision to be happy with his circumstances and made good use of his time by writing letters to churches. God inspired those letters so that they would become part of the Holy Scriptures that we read today.

God has provided all the resources necessary for us to make the right choices in life, so what guidelines can we follow in the decision-making process? Here are five important things to do.

1. Consult the Scriptures

The Bible is the clearest revelation we have of God's will, but it can be a dangerous book if it is wrongly interpreted. The Pharisees had Jesus crucified on the basis of their interpretation of the Old Testament Scriptures. The best interpreter of any book is the author, so no one can accurately interpret the Scriptures without the guidance of the Holy Spirit.

My wife and I were on vacation in Wyoming when we decided to go home earlier than planned. We caught a plane that took us to Salt Lake City, where we had to wait on standby. A group of five men on the standby list were also waiting in the airport. They lived in Georgia and were returning from an elk hunting trip in Canada. Fortunately, all seven of us were eventually seated on the plane.

Although I had never met him before, one of the hunters was about to teach a class on prayer in his church using a plan I had developed called *Prayer 101*. He had been praying for several weeks that God would show him how to teach it because he was confused about a few things. The group study would begin in four days, and he was getting nervous about leading the class.

I sat down next to him and introduced myself. "Hi, my name's Peter Lord."

The man stuck out his hand. "Good to meet you. I'm Clint. That's funny, I'm about to teach a book on prayer written by an author with the same name."

He almost fell out of his seat when I told him that I was the author of the book! God answered his prayer for further guidance by sending the author to him. For the next two hours, I explained how to teach the book and answered every question he had.

God the Father has sent the author of the Bible, the Holy Spirit, to help us interpret it. The Bible may not answer every question you have, but it does tell you how to get those answers. The Scriptures will give instructions on many of the decisions that you will need to make.

SECRET #1

God knows the best path for your life and is willing to reveal it to you.

Regarding marriage, for example, Christians are told to only marry other believers (see 1 Corinthians 7:40). Again, the Scripture tells us, "Do not be bound together with unbelievers" (2 Corinthians 6:14). What if you are already married to an unbeliever? God's Word gives instructions in that case as well: "If any brother has a wife who is an unbeliever, and she consents to live with him, he must not divorce her" (1 Corinthians 7:12).

In other places, the Bible gives examples of those who made certain choices, and we would be wise to follow their lead. In Acts 15, the apostles and elders gathered together to discuss some important issues. They reached a decision and said, "It seemed good to us" (verse 25) and "it seemed good to the Holy Spirit and to us" (verse 28). They reached a decision about what *seemed* right to them, after they had prayed and asked for God's guidance. Following their example, we can make decisions based on what seems like the right thing to do after prayer and consulting wise counselors.

The Scriptures also instruct us to pray for wisdom when we do not know what to do. James 1:5 says, "If any of you lack wisdom, let him ask of God, who gives to all generously and without reproach, and it will be given to him." This is a promise from God's Word that He will provide the guidance we need by speaking to our minds, if the answers are not already revealed in Scripture.

2. *Listen to the Holy Spirit*

The Holy Spirit, who is indwelling every believer, is called "the Helper" (John 16:7). He is called that because He will help us by leading us into the truth. In the letters to the seven churches in Revelation, Jesus says, "He who has an ear, let him hear what the Spirit says" (Revelation 2:29). The Bible gives us *general* guidance that is available to everyone, but the Holy Spirit can give you *specific* guidance concerning your situation. The Bible can tell you to marry a Christian, but the Holy Spirit can lead you to the right person to marry. The Spirit and the Word will always be in agreement.

When Jesus was getting ready to ascend into heaven, He told the disciples they would actually be better off when He left because the Holy Spirit would come to guide them. Jesus could only be in one place at a time because His human body limited Him, but the Holy Spirit is everywhere and with every believer. Because the Holy Spirit is one with Jesus, having the Holy Spirit in us is the same as having Jesus with us.

Jesus gave them hope for the sweet by-and-by by telling them that He was going to heaven to prepare a place for them. But He also gave them many promises for the nasty now-and-now. He promised to give us the Holy Spirit, who would come to guide us into all truth. He would be with us to lead us in every situation so we could make the right choices.

When we ask Jesus to save us, He enters in and dwells in our hearts (see Ephesians 3:17). Because He lives inside of us, He can now direct us from inside our hearts. So in what ways does He speak to us?

He Will Put Desires in Your Heart

Psalm 37:4 says, "Delight yourself in the Lord; and He will give you the desires of your heart." In other words, He will place the desire within your heart to want what He wants. That does not mean that everything you want is His will. It simply means that when you are completely submitted to Him, He will guide you through the desires He puts in your heart. Although wanting things sounds greedy, it is not selfish to want things if you are submitted to Him.

He Will Put Peace in Your Heart

Colossians 3:15 says, "Let the peace of Christ rule in your hearts." The Greek word for *rule* means "to act as an umpire" or "the one that decides." In sporting events, the umpire is the one who makes the decisions on close calls.

Suppose you are watching a baseball game and the count is three balls and two strikes. The pitcher throws the ball to the catcher, but the batter does not swing. The batter thinks it is ball four, while the catcher says it is strike three. They both look at the umpire who makes the call and decides whether the batter is out or if he goes to first base. God's peace does the same thing for us in that it directs us in how to proceed.

If you have no peace in your heart, God may be saying that what you are asking for is not in His will, or you may simply need to have some questions answered. Once you have received the answers, the peace should come. But if you still have no peace after receiving the answers, your decision is probably not His will, or the timing is wrong.

> A lack of peace in your heart may be a Holy Spirit warning that you are about to make a bad decision.

It is not wise to make decisions if you are experiencing turmoil inside your heart. A lack of peace in your heart may be the Holy Spirit warning that you are about to make a bad decision. God's peace in your heart is usually a confirmation that you are making a good choice.

He Will Put an Inner Knowing in Your Heart

"The Spirit Himself bears witness with our spirit that we are children of God" (Romans 8:16, NKJV). If God's Spirit bears witness with our spirit and lets us know that we are God's children, then He can also bear witness with us through an inner knowing.

An "inner knowing" is like having an intuition. Some people call it a "gut feeling" or a "holy hunch." I have heard other people say, "You know that you know that you know." It is knowledge that God puts inside your heart, and that is why the apostles and elders in Acts 15 could say, "It seemed good to the Holy Spirit and to us."

3. Get Advice from Wise Counselors

We cannot live the Christian life alone; it is a team sport. God will often use counselors to give us a greater amount of wisdom in making decisions. The Scriptures tell us that there is victory in the multitude of counselors. But do not choose just anyone to advise you. You must first make sure they are qualified before they counsel you.

First, make sure your advisors live godly lives. "Blessed is the man who walks not in the counsel of the ungodly" (Psalm 1:1, NKJV). If someone is not living like God wants, he or she will probably give you bad advice.

Next, your advisors should be experienced. "For by wise guidance you will wage war, and in abundance of counselors there is victory" (Proverbs 24:6). If you are going to wage war, do not go to your local mechanic for advice. Instead, listen to someone in the military who has fought battles and won. If you need advice about your car, however, listen to your mechanic, not a soldier. In other words, find someone who has experience in the area where you need to make a decision. Do not go to a person who cannot swim and ask him to teach you to swim. If he does not know how to do it, then it will not work for you either.

Finally, choose caring counselors. Former football coach Lou Holtz has said, "Don't tell your problems to people. Eighty percent don't care and the other twenty percent are glad you have them!" It is true that some people actually want you to fail, so make sure your counselors care about what happens to you if you take their advice.

Choose several advisors who are godly, caring and experienced, and it is likely they will give you good counsel. But remember, the final decision is your responsibility, not theirs.

4. Collect All Information about the Decision

It seems obvious that you should gather as much information as possible before you make a decision, but you would be surprised by how many people do not do this. Some people think it is a lack of faith to see if you can afford the item before you purchase it.

Look at what Jesus said about this.

> "For which one of you, when he wants to build a tower, does not first sit down and calculate the cost to see if he has enough to complete it? . . . Or what king, when he sets out to meet another king in battle, will not first sit down and consider whether he is strong enough with ten thousand men to encounter the one coming against him with twenty thousand?"
>
> Luke 14:28, 31

Jesus said the first thing you need to do when making a major decision is to sit down. This will keep you from running off and making a quick decision. To "sit down" means He wants you to take your time to think the decision through.

It is not wise to make a decision when you are emotionally high or emotionally low. When you are excited or depressed, it is hard to think realistically about a situation. Take enough time to let your emotions settle down so you can wisely evaluate the pluses and minuses. If God wants you to proceed, He will make it clear.

Next, Jesus instructed us to count the cost. Get out your calculator, a pencil and a piece of paper because you have some work to do. You have to think the decision through.

Let's see, I've got 10,000 soldiers and the other army has 20,000 soldiers. Hmmm. Let's go fight the battle! That would not be too smart. Do not go to war when you are outnumbered two to one. Do not buy a $50,000 car if you only make $100 a week.

Counting the cost means doing your homework. Remember, you are making an exchange, so you must think about what you are giving up versus what you will receive. To make a wise decision, here is what you will need to do:

- Gather all the facts before you make a decision.
- Consider the outcome for all scenarios.
- Look at the situation from every angle and perspective.
- Weigh every option. What will happen if you follow option A? What will happen with option B?
- Will you be happy with your decision two years from now?
- Leave no stone unturned. Check out everything.

Abraham's nephew Lot decided to move his family to Sodom without thinking his decision through. He lifted his eyes up and saw the valley was green, so it looked like a good place for his livestock (see Genesis 13:10–11). That one detail alone was enough to convince him it was the right place to live. He forgot to consider all the other factors in that situation. He soon found out the people in the city were exceedingly wicked.

Lot's biggest mistake was not collecting all information about the situation to begin with. If he had done that, he would never have made his home in Sodom.

If you are thinking about moving to another city, have you done your homework? Have you checked out the unemployment rate, churches, schools, crime rate, cost of living, and taxes? If you do not get the answers before you move, you will find out after you get there, but then it will be too late.

Once you have collected information about your potential situation, you need to compare it with your present situation—and then weigh the pluses and minuses of both situations. If you are married, you and your spouse need to make these decisions together. Husbands and wives often see things from different perspectives, which is actually a benefit to making the right choice.

5. *Walk in the Light That God Has Given You*

When God led Israel through the wilderness, Scripture tells us, "The pillar of cloud did not leave them by day, to guide them on their way, nor the pillar of fire by night, *to light for them the way in which they were to go*" (Nehemiah 9:19, emphasis added). Although God does not lead us in exactly the same way today, He still guides us by illuminating our paths.

Walk in the light you have, even if it is only a flicker. He may be shining just enough light on your path to take one step. As you take that step, He will give light for another step, and so on.

When you are driving at night, you do not see the entire highway lit up all at once. You can only see how far your car's headlights will shine down the road. But as your car moves, the light keeps shining ahead of you.

In the same way, as you walk in faith by what God has revealed, He will continue to give you light so you can travel on the right path. God says, "I will instruct you and teach you in the way which you should go" (Psalm 32:8).

Better Choices Make for a Better Life

Your life will be radically changed for better or worse by the choices you make. But what about the bad choices you have already made? Can God still lead you?

God is certainly aware of the mistakes you have made, and through His grace He can work your current circumstances into His will. The Lord works with every repentant person in his or her current situation, no matter how bad it may be. A former prostitute said, "The best lesson I learned is that my past does not have to be my future."

You have the responsibility to make better choices, beginning today. What do you want out of life? You get to decide. It is your choice.

Discussion Questions

Deciding to Decide

Reflecting on your life, what was a good decision that you made? What was a bad decision?

Besides Esau trading his birthright, what are some other "trades" people in the Bible made? What was the outcome of their decisions?

Read Galatians 6:7. How does this verse apply to consequences?

What are the three ways the Holy Spirit will confirm His will in your heart?

How can consulting with wise counselors help you make decisions?

Read Luke 14:28–32. When making a decision, why should you sit down and count the cost?

What does it mean to "walk in the light God has given you"?

CHALLENGE #2

OVERCOMING TEMPTATIONS

I can resist everything but temptation.

—Oscar Wilde

A friend of mine, who was a well-respected building inspector, had to inspect a building that was owned by a highly influential person in town. He could not approve the structure because it did not meet code and needed a number of very expensive major corrections to pass inspection.

Not long after this, my friend received some subtle threats and was told if he wanted to keep his job, he needed to approve the project without requiring any changes.

Now he had a dilemma. His job was his livelihood, yet he did not want to compromise his integrity. It would be easy for him to simply ignore the code violations. No one would ever know, except for God.

My friend refused to yield to the temptation and told the influential man that he had to make the improvements to pass the inspection. A couple of days later, my friend lost his job.

Just as my friend was tempted to compromise, so will you also be tempted. Never forget that by giving in to temptation, you can destroy in five minutes a reputation, a marriage or a ministry that it took years to build. It helps to understand a couple of facts about Challenge #2.

First, God does not tempt anyone. The desires of your own flesh cause the temptation, not God.

> Let no one say when he is tempted, "I am being tempted by God"; for God cannot be tempted by evil, and He Himself does not tempt anyone. But each one is tempted when he is carried away and enticed by his own lust.
>
> James 1:13–14

Second, just because you are tempted does not mean that you have sinned. Sin is yielding to temptation. Jesus was tempted in all things, just as we are; yet He did not sin (see Hebrews 4:15). Although He was tempted to the maximum in every area, He never gave in to it.

Five Basic Drives

Temptation works through the drives and desires that God created within you. Some of the primary ones are your hunger drive, sex drive, fellowship drive, approval drive and worship drive. All these are legitimate drives and God has provided an acceptable way to fulfill them.

If you keep giving in to temptations, they can amplify your desires so that they become an obsession. A person hooked on pornography keeps feeding that drive, and when a drive is overfed it becomes an *addiction*. Whenever you fulfill a drive in a bizarre or twisted way, it becomes a *perversion*. Listed below is a description of some of the God-created impulses within us:

Hunger Drive. We all need to eat, so this one does not need an explanation. When we magnify this drive, we eat more food than we should and it turns into gluttony. Eating disorders, such as anorexia nervosa or bulimia, are perversions of the hunger drive. If we do not control this drive, it will control us.

Sex Drive. God told Adam and Eve, "Be fruitful and multiply, and fill the earth" (Genesis 1:28). The Lord created this drive for reproduction and pleasure, but only within the covenant of marriage. God's ideal plan is for a man and woman to be virgins when they get married. Many people try to fulfill this drive in forbidden ways through fornication, adultery, pornography, homosexuality and bestiality. If you are involved in any of these perversions, you must ask God to forgive you and deliver you from their power.

Fellowship Drive. "The LORD God said, 'It is not good for the man to be alone; I will make him a helper suitable for him'" (Genesis 2:18). Adam was alone because his need for fellowship was not being fulfilled, so God created the woman to fulfill not only his sex drive, but also his need for social interaction.

Approval Drive. This impulse can become so strong that a person will do almost anything to gain approval. On the other hand, some people will suppress this drive because they do not care what anyone else thinks. We can legitimately fulfill this drive when we seek God's approval above all else. Some of the Jewish leaders "loved the approval of men rather than the approval of God" (John 12:43).

Worship Drive. Within everyone is a need to worship someone or something. The Greek word for worship means "to kiss toward." If we do not worship the true God, we will pervert this yearning by worshipping idols—sports, hobbies, money, celebrities, or some other fixation. You can identify what you worship by examining your greatest passion and what receives your attention, time and money.

The Temptation Process

When we examine how Adam and Eve were tempted, it helps us understand the temptation process and our own struggles. The steps listed below concern the hunger drive, but the same principles apply to all the drives inside us.

> **When a drive is overfed it becomes an addiction.**

Step #1: Our Hunger Drive Craves Food

God could have created Adam without a need to eat, which would have kept him from eating the forbidden fruit. Instead, the Lord gave him a mouth, a stomach and a hunger drive. The hunger drive caused him to *want* to eat and to look for a way to fulfill his appetite.

Then the Lord placed Adam in the Garden filled with trees bearing fruit so Adam could satisfy his craving. The fruit from those trees would be the legitimate way for Adam to fulfill his hunger.

> The LORD God commanded the man [Adam], saying; "From any tree of the garden you may eat freely; but from the tree of the knowledge of good and evil you shall not eat, for in the day you eat from it you will surely die."
>
> Genesis 2:16–17

God placed the Tree of Knowledge of Good and Evil in the Garden and commanded Adam and Eve not to eat from it. The fruit on this tree was forbidden and off-limits to them. God prohibited them from fulfilling their hunger drive by eating from this tree.

Temptation is trying to fulfill a legitimate drive in an illegitimate way. It is attempting to fulfill our needs and desires in ways that God does not sanction.

Satan attacked Jesus through His hunger drive when he tempted Him in the wilderness.

> Then Jesus was led up by the Spirit into the wilderness to be tempted by the devil. And after He had fasted forty days and forty nights, He then became hungry. And the tempter came and said to Him, "If you are the Son of God, command that these stones become bread."
>
> Matthew 4:1–3

The devil began tempting Jesus *after* He became hungry. Satan wanted to tempt Him though His hunger drive, which needed to be fulfilled. He suggested a quick solution to the problem: Jesus could turn some rocks into bread. When you are starving, the devil can make unappealing things look attractive. Even rocks begin to look good!

Temptation is trying to fulfill a legitimate drive in an illegitimate way.

Satan probably pointed to a stone that looked exactly like a loaf of bread. If Jesus really had the miracle-working powers of the Son of God, He could have simply rearranged the molecules. All He needed to do was to look at the rock and say, "Change." The devil suggested to Jesus that He should fulfill His hunger drive by using His God-given powers, even if it meant disobeying His Father.

Jesus knew He had the power to do it because He did His first miracle by rearranging the molecules in water and making it into wine. The Father, however, never told Him to change the stones into bread, so it would have been an illegal way for Him to satisfy His hunger.

Step #2: We Decide to Examine the Forbidden Fruit

When did the temptation begin for Adam and Eve? It did not begin when they were at the tree looking at the fruit. The temptation began when they *decided* to go to the middle of the garden to look at the fruit. Temptation starts when we make that first step to examine forbidden fruit.

The alcoholic enters into temptation when he decides to go to the bar, not after he arrives. The enticement starts when you decide to click on that link to the Internet site. The temptation begins when you make the decision to do something that God forbids.

Jesus taught us to pray, "Do not lead us *into* temptation" (Matthew 6:13, emphasis added). Temptation covers an area that can be entered into. When Jesus was in the Garden of Gethsemane, He told His disciples, "Keep watching and praying that you may not enter *into* temptation" (Matthew 26:41, emphasis added).

The Greek word to go "into" something means to move from the outside to the inside, like being on the outside of a house and going through a doorway to get inside. You enter into temptation through an entrance door. When Adam and Eve were away from the tree, they were not being tempted by it. But when they took that first step toward the illegal tree, they went through the door of temptation and entered *into* temptation.

Something happens to you when you go through that door. Suddenly the power of the temptation starts pulling on you. Once you enter that area, you come "under the influence" of the temptation.

Entering into Temptation

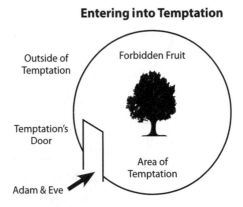

When you are outside of the temptation, you must make up your mind not to go inspect forbidden fruit. Purpose in your heart ahead of time that you will not click on that link to a porn site. When someone invites you to go to a place where you will be tempted with drinking, drugs or sex, you should have already decided ahead of time that you are not going there.

Once you enter into temptation you will start warring inside. "Abstain from fleshly lusts which wage war against the soul" (1 Peter 2:11). Temptation is when your soul is at war. Some people constantly fall into sin because they keep going through the doors that lead to forbidden fruit.

Step #3: We Taste the Prohibited Fruit and Our Eyes Are Opened to It

When Adam and Eve arrived at the middle of the garden, Satan was waiting for them. How did he know to be waiting next to the forbidden fruit? The devil knew that was the place where Adam and Eve could be tempted. Satan knows to hang around places of temptation, where he can drop ideas into our minds to take a closer look at a forbidden object.

The serpent told Eve, "For God knows that in the day you eat from it your eyes will be opened" (Genesis 3:5). The devil tells us that yielding to the temptation will benefit us and make us happy.

> When the woman saw that the tree was good for food, and that it was a delight to the eyes, and that the tree was desirable to make one wise, she took from its fruit and ate; and she gave also to her husband with her, and he ate. Then the *eyes of both of them were opened.*
>
> Genesis 3:6–7, emphasis added

When they ate the forbidden fruit, their eyes were opened. This verse is not describing their physical eyes being opened because Scripture tells us she *saw* the tree was good for food and it was a delight to her *eyes.* Until that moment, Adam and Eve only knew good because they had not sinned. But the moment they disobeyed God and tasted the forbidden fruit, the eyes of their souls were opened to evil. Now they knew evil by experience. Once you have tasted a particular forbidden fruit, your eyes have been opened to it.

I know a mother who has never let her two-year-old son eat chocolate. When they are at the grocery store, the boy does not cry for a chocolate bar at the checkout line like the other small children who are screaming for it. His eyes have never been opened to chocolate, so he does not know what it tastes like.

If you have never smoked cigarettes, your eyes have never been opened to it, so you do not know what it is like to be addicted to nicotine. If you have never taken drugs, you have not experienced the brief ecstasy that hooks people to it, or the ongoing cravings for a fix that a dope addict endures.

You are much better off if your eyes are not opened to some things! Contrary to popular belief, you do not have to personally experience everything this world has to offer. Temptation has a much greater pull on those whose eyes have been opened to a particular sin than on those who are innocent.

Step #4: We Become Addicted to Forbidden Fruit

Sin is fun at first. It satisfies a need for the moment, but the end result is what happens later. Satan always offers his best at the beginning and then it goes downhill after that.

The most delicious bite of the forbidden fruit is the first one, and we think the pleasure will continue with the second bite. We discover it is not quite as tasty as the first bite. So we take a third bite, trying to experience the thrill of the first one. As we keep taking more bites, we find the enjoyment diminishes but the compulsion to eat increases. Before we know it, we are addicted to the forbidden fruit.

All forbidden fruit has a hook buried inside. When a fisherman goes fishing, he is trying to deceive the fish into thinking it is getting a free meal. When the fish bites on a juicy worm, he does not realize that a hook is hidden inside. The next thing he knows, he is being pulled out of the water. He flops around in vain, trying to get back into the water. Soon he is sizzling in a frying pan and finally ends up in the fisherman's stomach. When he was underwater lusting after that worm, he never dreamed he would end up as a meal.

All temptations are traps. The alcoholic who lost his job and family never dreamed it would happen when he took his first drink. If everyone could see the disastrous consequences of taking the bait, no one would ever yield. No mouse would ever nibble on that cheese in the mousetrap.

Temptation Corner

Temptation is like coming to a street corner. It is a dividing line, where you must choose one of two directions. You can either take God's way or your own way, but you cannot take both. Here are seven keys to gaining victory over temptation.

Key #1: Call on Your Higher Power

Your personal walk with Jesus Christ is the most important factor in overcoming temptation. You will need a power that is stronger than yourself to help you win this battle. The Alcoholics Anonymous program teaches alcoholics to call on their higher power when they are tempted. The Holy Spirit is your higher power and He gives you the supernatural ability to overcome temptation.

God tells us, "Walk by the Spirit, and you will not carry out the desire of the flesh" (Galatians 5:16). When you yield to the Holy Spirit in your daily walk, you are "walking in the Spirit." The only way to displace the desires of your flesh is through a genuine work of the Holy Spirit inside your heart.

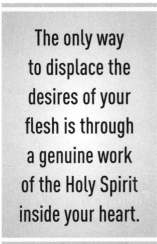

The only way to displace the desires of your flesh is through a genuine work of the Holy Spirit inside your heart.

The Holy Spirit and your flesh will pull you in opposite directions. "For the flesh sets its desire against the Spirit, and the Spirit against the flesh; for thesc arc in opposition to one another" (Galatians 5:17). The flesh will always pull you toward temptation, not away from it.

Every form of life has certain basic desires imbedded in it. Vultures have the natural desire to eat dead things. Ducks want to spend time in water. Pigs like to wallow in the mud. It is their nature that causes them to do those things.

So where does the desire for spiritual things come from? It is not going to come from your flesh. The motivation to please God only comes from the Holy Spirit, and yielding to Him is your only way to have victory over temptation.

Feed your spirit every day by reading God's Word and your spirit will get stronger. Who in their right mind would send out an army who hasn't eaten in a week to fight a battle? The soldiers would be too weak to fight. Feed your spirit and starve your flesh.

Key #2: Instead of Resisting the Temptation, Run Away from It

Most people try to resist temptation and that is why they lose. When you try to resist in the flesh, you will lose because the flesh actually wants to yield. The flesh is what got you into the temptation in the first place—and now it is trying to get you out of it! "The spirit is willing, but the *flesh is weak*" (Matthew 26:41, emphasis added). You need to find a better strategy than resisting.

Instead of trying to resist temptation, it is better to turn around and run away. "Flee from youthful lusts" (2 Timothy 2:22). You can break the pull of temptation if you will run away from it. You must exit the realm that you entered into.

Temptation is like a magnetic field. If a piece of iron is brought inside the magnetic field, the iron will be pulled and attracted to the magnet. But if you keep the iron outside the magnetic field, the iron will not be pulled to it because it is outside the field's sphere of influence.

Forbidden fruit also has a magnetic field. When you stay away from the object of temptation, you are outside the sphere of influence and you will not feel the magnetic pull toward it. Once you decide, however, to examine the forbidden object like Eve did, and start walking toward it, the pull becomes stronger with each step. You can break the magnetism if you turn around and run away from it, which will take you back outside the influence of the magnetic field. This is the way of escape.

God's Word makes this promise.

No temptation has overtaken you but such as is common to man; and God is faithful, who will not allow you to be tempted beyond what you are able, but with the temptation will provide *the way of escape* also.

1 Corinthians 10:13, emphasis added

God will always make a way out of the temptation, but you must look for it. You entered into the temptation through the entrance door, so the way out is to look for the exit door and run through it.

When Potiphar's wife tried to seduce Joseph, he didn't stand there, trying to resist her. Instead, he turned around and ran out through the exit door (see Genesis 39:12). Even though Adam and Eve were standing under the tree, they still had not sinned and could have gotten out away from it. All they had to do was turn around and run.

SECRET #2

Instead of resisting temptation, run from it.

Key #3: Fulfill Your Drives in God's Legitimate Way

God told Adam, "From any tree of the garden you may eat freely" (Genesis 2:16). He provided legitimate fruit for Adam to fulfill his hunger drive. If Adam and Eve had been eating the fruit that God had provided for them, they would not have been hungry for the forbidden fruit. God wants you to fulfill your needs and drives through His provision.

Suppose your family is gathered together for Thanksgiving and your mouth starts watering when you see homemade apple pie on the table. You are about to indulge yourself when your mother says, "You cannot eat that now. Lunch is ready. You can have it for dessert."

> If Adam and Eve had been eating fruit from the trees God had provided for them, they would not have been hungry for the forbidden fruit.

After eating two helpings of turkey and dressing with all the trimmings, you push yourself away from the table. You are so full that you have to loosen your belt. Then your mother comes out with a large piece of apple pie and places it in front of you.

You are repulsed at the sight of it and say, "Take it away. I'm full!"

Thirty minutes ago you were craving the pie, but now you cannot stand to look at it. What happened? Your hunger drive has been fulfilled, so the temptation is no longer there.

What works for your hunger drive also works for every other drive in you. If you fulfill your drives with God's legitimate fruit, you will not be hungry for forbidden fruit. But the reverse is also true. If you are eating forbidden fruit, you will not be hungry for God's fruit.

Key #4: Hang Around with the Right People

Just as you have a hunger drive, you also have a fellowship drive. You have a need to be with other people. You will become like the people you are around, and they will influence you to be better or worse. "He who walks with wise men will be wise, but the companion of fools will suffer harm" (Proverbs 13:20). If you do not fellowship with the right people, you will fellowship with the wrong people.

I poured my life into a young man years ago, trying to make him a disciple of Jesus. It seemed like my efforts were in vain when he walked away from God. He lost his job, dropped out of Christian fellowship, and began hanging out with the wrong crowd, which pulled him even further away. He was like a modern-day prodigal son, spending $70,000 on his drug habit. I kept pursuing him, even though he did everything to avoid me. But the love of God never gives up. Love does not say, "Well, I have tried for two years and he hasn't responded, so I am giving up." I kept praying that God would do something to change his heart.

He finally hit bottom and decided to get away from his drug addict friends. He checked in to a Christian drug and alcohol treatment ministry, where he started spending time with godly people. Through their help, he put some new disciplines into his life. He has been a pastor now for a number of years, and we see each other on a regular basis.

We become like the people we choose to be around. I started smoking at a very early age because of the company I admired and wanted to be with. They never tried to talk me into smoking, but they were doing it and I wanted to be like them.

The people we hang around with influence us, even if they do not openly seek to convert us to their ways of thinking. The pressure of the crowd operates like gravity—it controls some of our behavior, but we are not consciously aware it. The inbred desire to be accepted brings a pressure to conform to those around us.

It was not that long ago that only sailors and bikers had tattoos, but now it seems as though everyone is getting them, including girls and women. Yet, I have never seen an advertisement on television asking me to get a tattoo. People do it because the people they admire are wearing them. Their peers have influenced them.

One of the hardest pressures to resist comes from our peers. We all want to be accepted and approved by those around us.

You might not be able to avoid peer pressure, but you can choose your peers. If you hang around those who make wise choices, you will do the same. But fellowshipping with people who hate God will pull your heart away from Him. "You shall not associate with them, nor shall they associate with you, for they will surely turn your heart away after their gods" (1 Kings 11:2).

Key #5: Purpose in Your Heart to Stay Away from Forbidden Fruit

God did not put a fence around the forbidden fruit tree to keep Adam and Eve from getting near it. Instead of blocking their way to the fruit, He told them exactly where the tree was located, in the middle of the garden, so they could avoid it. It is easier to avoid temptation than it is to overcome it. If they had just stayed away from that place, they would not have been tempted by it.

Temptations typically begin with a thought to go to a certain place. Usually it is a private place where forbidden things can happen without anyone else knowing about them. By staying away from that place, you will stay out of trouble.

> It is hard to pick forbidden fruit from a hundred yards away, but it is easy to pick at an arm's length.

Adam and Eve decided to inspect the forbidden fruit. The closer they got to the tree, the more likely it was that they would eat from it. It is hard to pick forbidden fruit from a hundred yards away, but it is easy to pick at an arm's length.

The closer you get to the forbidden fruit, the weaker you will become. Superman gets weaker when he gets close to

Kryptonite, so he knows to stay away from that green rock. That is why you must decide *ahead of time* to keep away from the people and places where you are tempted. Distance makes a difference! If you will stay far away, you will be outside sin's influence.

Key #6: Think about the Consequences of Disobedience Ahead of Time

If we could only foresee the harmful consequences of eating forbidden fruit, it would deter us from doing a lot of things. The key to overcoming is to realize that temptations are not as delightful as they appear.

Dr. James Dobson once went deer hunting with his son. He put some corn in the middle of a field, and then they hid in some bushes. A deer showed up, took a long time cautiously looking around, and then began eating. Dr. Dobson told his boy, "Son, always remember, when you see free corn in the middle of a field, someone is getting ready to shoot you down."

Do not be deceived by innocent-looking entrapments. Envisioning the damaging consequences of yielding to temptation is a preventative measure that keeps us from falling into a snare.

Key #7: Regularly Meet with an Accountability Partner

Moses killed the Egyptian because he thought he could get away with it. "So he looked this way and that, and when he saw there was no one around, he struck down the Egyptian and hid him in the sand" (Exodus 2:12).

He looked "this way and that" because he wanted to make sure no one would see him commit the murder. We are most susceptible to fall into temptation when no one is looking. Having an accountability partner can solve that problem.

An "accountability partner" is a trusted, spiritually minded friend who cares about you. You voluntarily meet with this person on a regular basis. If you will confide in this individual, he or she will help you stay on the right path. If you know that you have to report to someone, it will make you think twice before making a wrong choice.

Michigan State University conducted a study and found that dieters who regularly reported to someone who monitored their weight loss had a 97 percent success rate. Those who did not report their weight loss to someone were only 20 percent successful. Having an accountability partner quadrupled their success rate.[1]

Ask someone that you trust to hold you accountable for the weak areas in your life. Meet with the person at least once a week and have that person ask you the tough questions.

The Reward for Overcoming

You may be wondering why you should take God's way instead of yielding. That is a valid question.

When you choose the right path, you will escape the painful consequences of sin, such as getting incurable sexually transmitted diseases. Avoiding temptation prevents addictions and serving time in prison. Every prisoner is in the penitentiary because they yielded to temptation.

Overcoming temptation also forms godly character within you and takes you to a new level of spiritual maturity. You will actually become stronger and wiser because of it, not to mention much happier. On Judgment Day, God also promises to give one of the greatest rewards to those who overcome temptation.

1. "Snippets," *Houston Chronicle* (pre-1997 Fulltext), June 26, 1996, http://ezproxy.hclib.org/login?url=http://search.proquest.com/docview/296126810?accountid=6743.

Blessed is the man who endures temptation; for when he has been approved, he will receive the crown of life which the Lord has promised to those who love Him.

James 1:12, NKJV

The crown of life is the "victor's crown" that will be one of our great eternal rewards in heaven.

I hope you will take this information and apply it to the temptations you face right now. You will be glad you did.

Discussion Questions

Avoiding Forbidden Fruit

Why did the devil tempt Jesus *after* He became hungry?

Why did God give Adam and Eve all the trees of the garden to eat from except one?

Discuss the statement: "Temptation is trying to fulfill a legitimate drive in an illegitimate way."

Why is it important to call on the Holy Spirit as your higher power?

How can fulfilling your drives in a legitimate way keep you from being tempted?

Why is fleeing from a temptation better than trying to resist it?

How can staying away from certain people and places keep you from being tempted?

CHALLENGE #3

DEVELOPING RELATIONSHIPS

If you want people to be glad to meet you, you must be glad
to meet them.

—Johann Wolfgang von Goethe

The third challenge addresses how to properly relate to others. We cannot function in this world until we understand
how relationships work. And it will not be easy. Someone
once said that everyone *has* a problem, *is* a problem, or *lives
with* one.

On your journey down life's highway, you are going to
meet various types of people. They will all think, act and
respond differently. Some people will be easy to get along
with, while others are difficult to be around. They will have
diverse personalities. Some have been wounded. Others
are downright mean. And God wants us to love every one
of them.

How can we live in these relationships for the glory of
God? This is an important question for the Christian, and

the way you answer is vitally important to fulfilling God's plan for your life, not to mention having happiness in this world.

The Pharisees once asked Jesus, "Teacher, which is the greatest commandment in the Law?" They had counted 613 commandments in the Law and wanted to know which was the most important.

Jesus answered:

> "You shall love the LORD your God with all your heart, and with all your soul, and with all your mind." This is the great and foremost commandment. The second is like it, "You shall love your neighbor as yourself."
>
> Matthew 22:36–39

God is more interested in relationships than anything else. In fact, He is more interested in us having right relationships than He is receiving our offerings. Jesus said:

> "Therefore if you are presenting your offering at the altar, and there remember that your brother has something against you, leave your offering there before the altar and go; first be reconciled to your brother, and then come and present your offering."
>
> Matthew 5:23–24

According to Jesus, the most important thing we can do is to love God with all our heart. If we are doing that, then we are also going to love all those people that He created, even if they seem strange or obnoxious.

> If someone says, "I love God," and hates his brother, he is a liar; for the one who does not love his brother whom he has seen, cannot love God whom he has not seen.
>
> 1 John 4:20

Everyone is on a search for love, and something is going to fill that void. A person without food will eventually eat anything. What people are looking for—and the only thing that will actually change them—is God's *agape* love. The Lord wants to use you to channel His love to others.

You must receive God's love before you can give it away. You cannot give away something that you do not have. You cannot give someone ten dollars until you have first received ten dollars and you are willing to let go of it. You cannot love your neighbor, your spouse, or your enemy until you have first received that love from God and you are willing to release it.

Foundational Truths

Many people choose to withdraw from all relationships, to stay in seclusion, and to keep to themselves. Perhaps someone has hurt them in the past and they do not want to be hurt like that again. The fact is, although it is risky to form relationships, withdrawing creates an even bigger problem—loneliness.

Loneliness is one of the most painful emotions that people can experience. In my sixty years as a pastor, I have seen so many people who were hurting from being alone. Even if you live with another person, you can still feel alone because you lack meaningful interaction. You can be lonely even when surrounded by a crowd.

God created us with a fellowship drive, which is a need to relate with others. Because He designed us to have relationships, we will feel a void inside if we do not interact. Although everything God created was good, He looked at Adam and said, "It is not good for the man to be alone" (Genesis 2:18). He set about correcting the problem by bringing a wife to Adam.

Before Eve was created, the Lord told Adam that he could eat from any tree in the Garden except for the Tree of Knowledge of Good and Evil. After God created Eve, perhaps Adam said, "God said to not eat from the tree. Just to be on the safe side, don't even touch it. Okay?"

When the devil tempted Eve, she told him, "God has said, 'You shall not eat from it *or touch it*, or you will die'" (Genesis 3:3, emphasis added). After she picked the fruit, she realized that she did not die from touching it, so what harm could there be in eating it? The fall of the human race began with miscommunication, and relationships continue to be destroyed for the same reason.

You must receive God's love before you can give it away.

Communication is more than talking. It is also listening, understanding what is being said and responding in an appropriate way. For relationships to work as God intends, good communication is vital.

Do not assume that you will never have a disagreement or conflict. Expecting too much from another person will create criticism and frustration. Unrealistic expectations are a setup for conflict to happen, so it is a good and healthy practice to lower your expectations of others.

Some relationships take priority over other relationships. Quality time is when you give your full attention to the other person. Spending time with your spouse needs to happen before you give time to your friends. A father needs to give his children quality time, which is more important than playing golf with a friend or watching television.

Not all relationships are meant to be at the same level. It is wise to know when we should and should not form a deeper association with someone.

Levels of Relationships

Relationships often progress. When you first get to know someone, it starts as a surface relationship. As you spend more time with that individual, the relationship can deepen, according to how much you are both willing to open up and share with each other. As you get to know a person in a deeper way, the commitment increases, which moves you to the next level.

Before you proceed any further with someone, take a close look at the other person's character and values. Are they the same as yours? If not, it would be wise not to go to a deeper level with that individual. Proverbs 13:20 says, "He who walks with wise men will be wise, but the companion of fools will suffer harm." In other words, you will become like the people you hang around with. Your friends will influence and shape you, so choose them very carefully.

All relationships will stall at the level where mutual sharing stops. Rapport is built on common interests, goals and mutual likes and dislikes. The more things people have in common, the stronger and deeper the relationship.

Relationships must be kept up and maintained. If neglected, they will deteriorate for sure. How do you keep them up? By doing the same things that built them up in the first place. The following six levels of relationships will reveal the depth that you can connect with others.

Level 1: Stranger (Shake Hands)

All relationships begin with someone we never knew before. Jesus said, "I was a stranger, and you invited Me in" (Matthew 25:35). In a church setting, a stranger might be someone who visits the church for the first time. When you introduce yourself, it is the starting point in developing a relationship. It may or may not proceed to the next level.

An *instrumental relationship* is an association that is formed through a product or service that is offered. An example of this would be my relationship with my plumber. I need my plumbing fixed and the repairman needs my money. He and I get along just fine, but if it were not for the plumbing and money, we would not even have a connection. We would never see each other unless I had a leaky pipe.

Notice in the illustration (page 64) that the Stranger level is the outside ring, and it contains the most people. You can have far more people in level one than any other type of relationship.

Level 2: Acquaintance (Share Facts)

When Jesus was twelve years old, His family was returning home from the Passover Feast in Jerusalem. Joseph and Mary had traveled a day's journey and thought Jesus was in the caravan. When they realized He was not there, "they began looking for Him among their relatives and acquaintances" (Luke 2:44).

An acquaintance is someone you have met, but you do not know on a deep level. At this level, you *share facts* with each other. You find out where the person works, or some facts about their family. You ask about the person's hobbies or favorite football team.

> All relationships will stall at the level where mutual sharing stops.

This is at best a very superficial relationship. You have learned some facts about the other person, but you really do not know an acquaintance very well. You have no obligations or expectations of each other, but if you want to know this person better, you move to the next level.

Levels of Relationships

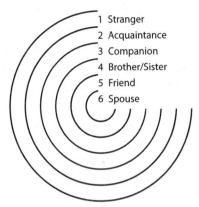

1 Stranger
2 Acquaintance
3 Companion
4 Brother/Sister
5 Friend
6 Spouse

Level 3: Companion (Share Opinions)

Acts 13:13 tells us, "Now Paul and his companions put out to sea." Paul did not take acquaintances out to sea, but his companions. At this level, you *share opinions*. You say to a companion, "I believe this" or "Here is what I think."

At this level of the relationship, you are usually attracted to them and desire to get to know them on a deeper level. You do things together such as playing golf, shopping together or having coffee. You begin asking the "what do you think" questions.

You might ask how they feel about a particular issue or their political persuasion. These questions can be risky and may even determine whether the relationship halts or continues. It is at this level that you start discovering your differences, and may even start arguing.

If you enjoy the other person's personality and have a good time with them, the relationship will likely continue and possibly go deeper. If you do not like something about the other person, however, or if you strongly disagree with their opinions, the relationship will likely end. Those who are highly opinionated may back away because agreement with their opinions is more important to them than keeping the relationship.

To go to the next level of relationship, you must agree to disagree with the other person. Keeping the relationship intact must become more important to you than agreement on every opinion and issue. This is where you can mature in your faith and learn to accept people who do not believe everything that you do.

Remember that opinions are different than convictions. We will die for a conviction, but not for an opinion. Convictions should be built on biblical principles, while your upbringing, culture and what you have been taught form your opinions. In many cases, holding to a biblical conviction is a valid reason to halt a relationship with someone who is hostile toward the Lord.

The companion level has no real inner connection or soul ties. These relationships come and go, and when they go, there is no real sense of loss because they were superficial.

Take another look at the diagram. As the relationship goes toward a deeper level, you move toward the center of the circle and the rings get smaller. With each deeper level, the number of people who can fit inside each ring becomes fewer.

Level 4: Brother or Sister (Share Emotions)

"Brothers . . . bear one another's burdens" (Galatians 6:1–2, ESV). At this level, you *share emotions*. You open up and share your hurts and struggles. This is where intimacy begins. I want you to know me as I really am and what I am about.

This kind of relationship is developed through ties: family ties, soul ties, business ties, social ties, value ties and enjoyment ties. Both parties enjoy and benefit by the relationship because a bond is being formed. These are the people we choose to be with when we can choose. Each enjoys the other and the time together is beneficial to both.

It is not necessary to agree on every opinion and issue. It is important, however, to be in agreement on your belief in God, the teachings of the Bible and your basic philosophy of life. When this happens, a connection takes place.

The degree of real bonding will depend on the commonalities of both parties, and the amount of mutual sharing between them. They will share their dreams, desires, goals, convictions, enjoyments, ideas, commitments, concerns, values and burdens.

Here are some things to look for if the relationship is going to be beneficial and lasting:

- Ability to disagree agreeably.
- Understanding the blessing of diversity.
- Realizing that I cannot see everything from my vantage point.
- Bonding together; a feeling of belonging and togetherness.
- Mutual enjoyment of the relationship.
- Serving each other in various ways.
- Knowing the difference between an opinion and a conviction, and not always seeking to change the other's opinions, but giving respect.

Separation at this level and the next two levels cannot take place without pain and some loss because real connections are being severed.

Level 5: Friend (Share Secrets)

Proverbs 17:17 says, "A friend loves at all times." If you have a relationship with someone who is always mad at you, he or she is not a friend. If someone is putting you in bondage, that is not a friend either. A friend loves at all times.

At this level, you *share secrets*. I am not talking about sharing gossip or smearing another person's reputation and saying, "Do not tell anyone." It is revealing those things that are closest to your heart.

Some things you cannot share with just anyone. Not many people can keep a secret. You cannot reveal secret things to someone until you first establish a level of trust. A real friend will not run out telling everyone what you have said or do things to hurt you.

Now look at how small that circle is on the diagram. You can have very few friends at this level. "A man of too many friends comes to ruin" (Proverbs 18:24). Why? You do not have the time or energy to be a close friend to a lot of people. You can be friendly to everyone, but you only have time to handle a few friends, so choose them wisely.

Friendship requires a great deal of time and effort to develop and maintain. Jonathan and David in the Old Testament were an example of this. They made a covenant to protect each other, even though Jonathan's father wanted to kill David.

Here are some unique signs that you are at this level.

- You realize and accept the value of constructive criticism.
- Mutual accountability is wanted and practiced.
- You have a deep level of trust with no fear of being betrayed.
- You have the same basic purpose and destination in life.
- You both speak the truth in love. "Faithful are the wounds of a friend, but deceitful are the kisses of an enemy" (Proverbs 27:6).
- You can open your heart, knowing they will give you advice if they can, but will be honest if they do not know.

Level 6: Spouse (Share Everything)

Only two people can fit inside the innermost circle in the diagram. Jesus said when people get married, "The two shall become one" (Mark 10:8). This is the closest oneness possible on a human level. Two people cannot become one unless they *share everything*. When two people enter the covenant of marriage, they vow to each other, "Everything I have is yours."

I knew a married couple who kept a list of every item in their house and split it up as his and hers. If they purchased a couch, they wrote it down on her "mine" list. If they bought a television, they recorded it on his "mine" list. They did this with every valuable and piece of furniture in their home. When asked why they did this, they explained, "If we ever get a divorce, we will know exactly how to split it up by getting out the list."

When they got married, they never truly made a commitment to share everything. Can you guess what happened? They got a divorce. Sadly, they had no problem splitting up their stuff.

Many marriages do not last because couples go from being strangers (level 1) to acquaintances (level 2), and they barely make it to level 3 before jumping to level 6. They do not take enough time to really get to know each other. They never work through the other levels. They never learn how to share opinions or how to agree to disagree. They never learn how to share emotions in a healthy way. They never become friends.

If you rushed into getting married, God can still bless your marriage if you will work through and develop all the levels of your relationship. Learn to share opinions and emotions in a good way. Make sure your spouse is your best friend. Good friends have things in common and enjoy being with each other. The more things you have in common, the stronger and better your relationship will be.

God wants husbands and wives to be united. "Can two walk together, unless they are agreed?" (Amos 3:3, NKJV). Agreed on what? Where they want to go. Unity brings great power and that is why God wants to unite husbands and wives to accomplish His purposes.

In contrast, the devil's primary strategy has always been to divide and conquer, whether it is churches, marriages, or minds. Jesus declared, "Any kingdom divided against itself is laid waste; and any city or house divided against itself will not stand" (Matthew 12:25). Satan tries to divide a marriage by magnifying their differences and ignoring their commonalities.

Of course, even happily married couples will have some differences, but these are usually the superficial areas of life and are not really that important. Here are some important points of agreement for married couples:

- Going to the same place to worship God.
- Agreement in the ways to operate in life, such as how to handle money.
- Union of body, soul and spirit.
- Having the same life purpose.

The Principle of Deposits and Withdrawals

No matter what level of relationship you have with others, God wants you to treat them with kindness. Christ said, "Treat others the same way you want them to treat you" (Luke 6:31).

Your relationships work like a bank account where you make deposits and withdrawals. When you put money into an account, it is called a deposit. When you take money out of an account, it is a withdrawal. To retain a good relationship with your bank, your deposits must *precede* and *exceed* your withdrawals. If you do not make more deposits than withdrawals, you will get into trouble with your bank.

> By making more withdrawals than deposits, the relationship changes from replenishing to draining.

In the same way, you have a relationship bank account with others, where you are making deposits and withdrawals. Deposits are those pleasant and friendly interactions with others. When you smile at someone, you are making a deposit. When you speak kind words or encourage someone, you are depositing in that person. Giving gifts and helping others are other ingredients for a good relationship.

Withdrawals are just the opposite of deposits. These are angry and hurtful interactions with others. When you argue, criticize, or make cutting remarks, you are making withdrawals, which will have a negative effect on other people.

The health of your relationship with another person is determined by the amount of deposits and withdrawals you make. As long as you are making more deposits than withdrawals, you are going to have a positive rapport with that person. But if you are making more withdrawals than deposits (or someone is making more withdrawals from you), you are going to have a negative, strained relationship with that person. The amount of deposits and withdrawals will produce two kinds of relationships.

A *draining relationship* is when someone is withdrawing more than they are depositing. It is usually identified by continual friction, conflict and arguing. This kind of relationship will sap the energy and joy out of you until the fuel gauge reads empty.

A *replenishing relationship* is when someone is making more deposits than withdrawals. Although there may be a few withdrawals from time to time, a greater number of deposits outweigh the withdrawals. In a replenishing relationship, you will enjoy being with that person.

A marriage gets in trouble when it turns into a draining relationship marked by arguing and friction. Of course, it did not start out that way. It began as a replenishing relationship where the man and woman enjoyed spending time together.

They went on dates and talked on the phone for hours. They ran through the fields of flowers together, holding hands and laughing. They gazed into each other's eyes and said, "This is so wonderful. We need to get married and spend the rest of our lives together!" And so they did.

But not long after exchanging the wedding vows, they quit running through the fields of flowers together laughing. They stopped dating, holding hands and sending love notes to each other. They *stopped* making deposits into each other's accounts.

Soon, they started making withdrawals by getting into arguments over little things. Rather than saying how much they loved each other, they started yelling and slamming doors. By making more withdrawals than deposits, the relationship changed from replenishing to draining. If they keep withdrawing more than they deposit, the marriage will eventually go bankrupt, which is called divorce.

The good news is that a draining relationship can be turned back into a replenishing relationship simply by increasing the deposits in the other person's account and stopping the withdrawals.

How to Build a Replenishing Relationship

Some people are nice to us, while others can be hateful. We wish that everyone would be kind to us, which causes us to reciprocate with kindness. Jesus calls us to a higher level of behavior. He said:

> "If you love those who love you, what credit is that to you? For even sinners love those who love them. If you do good to those who do good to you, what credit is that to you? For even sinners do the same."
>
> Luke 6:32–33

Jesus expects His followers to go beyond the natural responses that even a lost person can exhibit. He wants us to act and react in ways that can only be fulfilled through His *agape* love, which can only come from God Himself.

Our interactions with others can be either proactive or reactive. When we are reactive, the other person instigates words or actions toward us, which call for us to respond in some way. Being proactive means that we initiate our actions based on scriptural principles and values, regardless of how another person acts toward us.

Jesus gave us both proactive and reactive commands. He gave a reactive command when He said, "Whoever hits you on the cheek, offer him the other also; and whoever takes away your coat, do not withhold your shirt from him either" (Luke 6:29).

Turning the other cheek is not a normal human reaction. Nothing inside us wants to react kindly when someone mistreats us. To respond correctly, we must act on His instructions and allow His Spirit to react appropriately through us. Without His enablement, we cannot respond in the way He wants.

Jesus gave a proactive command when He said, "Love your enemies, and do good, and lend, *expecting nothing in return*; and your reward will be great" (Luke 6:35, emphasis added). Notice that we do not do these things to receive something back. To compensate us in a better way, God promises to reward us—either in this life, the next, or both, if we will just do what He says.

The New Testament contains 26 reciprocal commands using the phrase "one another," which indicates that both parties need to be active. Nineteen of these commands are positive things we need to do. Seven commands are negative, which are things we should not do if we want good relationships. Following these reciprocal commands does not just strengthen marriages, but every relationship where both parties are obeying God with a loving heart.

Keep these proactive and reactive concepts in mind as you read about how to build a replenishing relationship with someone. Only by God's grace will you act and react appropriately in your situation.

Principle #1: When Someone Makes a Withdrawal Out of You, Do the Opposite and Make a Deposit in Them

God wants you to react with the opposite spirit. Jesus said, "Love your enemies, do good to those who hate you, bless those who curse you, pray for those who mistreat you" (Luke 6:27–28). Rather than reacting in the same spirit, do the opposite.

When people hate you (withdrawal), do good to them (deposit).

When people curse you (withdrawal), bless them (deposit).

When people mistreat you (withdrawal), pray for them (deposit).

The apostle Paul said:

> "If your enemy is hungry, feed him [deposit], and if he is thirsty, give him a drink [deposit]; for in so doing you will heap burning coals on his head." Do not be overcome by evil [withdrawal], but overcome evil with good [deposit].
>
> Romans 12:20–21

Instead of fighting back, react in the opposite spirit and make a deposit. You cannot fight fire with fire; you must use water. If you will obey God and do the opposite, He will start convicting the other person to change.

A friend of mine said he had the meanest mailman in the world. No one in the neighborhood liked him. One time my friend parked his car a little too close to the mailbox, so the postman decided to not deliver mail that day.

One day, as my friend's wife was praying, the thought popped into her mind to bake some brownies for the malicious mailman. That day, when he walked up to deliver the mail, they greeted him by saying, "We just want to thank you for your hard work in faithfully delivering our mail." Then they handed him the brownies.

For the first time since they had lived there, the mailman's face lit up with a big smile. He said, "Hey, it is not a problem. Thanks for the brownies."

My friend said that after giving him the brownies, he became the friendliest mailman he ever had. Whenever he was driving down the street, the postman would wave at him with a big grin on his face.

What changed him from being mean to nice? They made a deposit into his bankrupt account by doing something kind to him. Until he received some love, he could not respond in the right way. If they had not decided to treat him with kindness, it is unlikely that he would have changed his attitude toward them.

You cannot change a husband or wife in a positive way by yelling, nagging, or giving a cold shoulder. A person's behavior will not change until his or her heart changes. The transformation in the other person will happen as a result of you making deposits into this individual, along with the convicting work of the Holy Spirit.

Principle #2: Deposits Must Be in a Currency Acceptable to the Other Person's Bank

My bank will not accept ceramic ducks as deposits. If I take Mexican pesos to my bank, they will not accept that either. My bank only takes United States currency.

If you want to create a replenishing relationship, you must find out what kind of currency other people will accept in their banks, and it may not be the same currency that you like to receive. Deposits must be in the currency acceptable in the other person's bank, not your own.

Find out what the other person likes to receive. My wife does not care for sports, but she likes flowers. Why she likes flowers instead of sports I will never know, because my bank does not accept flowers as deposits.

A number of years ago, a lady said some very unkind things about my church and me. As she continued to create strife, I decided to invite her and her husband to our house to see if we could resolve the conflict.

A person's behavior will not change until his or her heart changes.

After talking though issues, she apologized for the things she had said. I told her, "Please let me take you and your husband out to lunch." I was trying to show that I had accepted their apologies, but I also knew the importance of making deposits in their bank account. I took them both to lunch and later I bought her a gift that she liked. Now she is always nice to me whenever we meet.

As you keep making the right kind of deposits, the balance in the other person's account will increase. The other person will probably become friendlier toward you as a result of your unconditional kindness.

Principle #3: God Will Give You the Ability to Make Deposits in Others

Some people say, "I just cannot do it. It is just too hard to make deposits."

That is just not true. God commands you to love your enemies, and He will never tell you to do something that He will not also enable you to do. God will always give you the ability to do His will.

SECRET #3

Build your relationships by making more deposits in others than withdrawals.

Until you forgive the person who hurt you, it will be impossible to make a deposit in that individual. If you do not forgive, you will become bitter, which is the most dangerous condition you could possibly have.

Forgiveness is simply releasing the anger and hostility out of your heart. You give up the wish to punish them or get even. You let go of vengeance and receive God's peace into your heart. You will know that you have forgiven when you are not angry anymore, when you have stopped talking about how much they hurt you.

Take a step of faith and do something nice for someone. Do it because you love God. Do it with the expectation that the Lord will use it to change the person's heart. And do not get upset if you do not see immediate results. Sometimes change takes place a little bit at a time.

Now you know what is necessary to develop relationships. But what if you are faced with a conflict that is difficult to resolve? We will talk about that in the next chapter.

Discussion Questions

Examining Your Bank

Read Proverbs 13:20. How are you influenced by the people you fellowship with?

What is the difference between a conviction and an opinion?

For people to go deeper in a relationship, they must agree to disagree. How can the boundary lines be drawn to make this happen?

What does it mean to share secrets without gossiping?

What is the difference between a draining relationship and a replenishing relationship?

If relationships are like a bank account, why do many marriages get into trouble?

Read Luke 6:27–28. What does Jesus say to do when people make withdrawals?

Why does the currency need to be acceptable to the other person's bank and not your own bank?

Challenge #4

RESOLVING CONFLICTS

Have you ever noticed that the people who tell you to calm down are the ones who upset you in the first place?

—Maxine

Someone once said that when two or three are gathered together in His name, you can count on one of them starting an argument. Wherever there are people, there will also be conflicts. This fourth challenge is the result of something going wrong with a relationship, as mentioned in the previous chapter.

A certain lady in our town did not like me. Even when I reached out to her, she would not speak to me. How do you resolve conflict with someone who refuses to talk to you?

She was a schoolteacher, so I wrote her a letter, saying that I had heard that she was a good teacher and had helped many students. I continued writing these notes of praise, not knowing how she would respond. As a result of my letters, her heart softened, and now she is always kind toward me.

All throughout the Bible we find people who could not get along. Abram's and Lot's herdsmen squabbled over territory (see Genesis 13:7). Jacob and Laban had continual conflicts in their dealings with each other (see Genesis 29–31). The disciples got into an argument over which one was the greatest (see Luke 22:24). That argument is still going on today in many circles. Even the apostles Paul and Barnabas had a sharp disagreement that caused them to separate (see Acts 15:38–39).

A conflict is a disagreement that produces friction and strained relationships between individuals. Friction comes from rubbing people the wrong way. To stop the tension in a relationship, both parties must stop fighting about their differences and agree to disagree.

The causes of conflict are too numerous to list. A difference of opinion is certainly the biggest reason. Clashing personalities, not listening, hot tempers, miscommunication, broken trust and selfishness are also guaranteed to create tension between individuals. All of these things, if not resolved, will produce damaging consequences—divorces, church splits and hurt feelings.

The Bible calls conflict "strife," which means "to quarrel, to cause discord." Some people seem to go out of their way to create trouble. "Like charcoal to hot embers and wood to fire, so is a contentious man to kindle strife" (Proverbs 26:21).

Not all strife can be avoided, but much of it can. The book of Proverbs reveals some of the things that create strife, as seen in the following verses:

> **Lying:** "[The Lord hates] a false witness who utters lies, and one who spreads strife among brothers" (Proverbs 6:19).

Hatred: "Hatred stirs up strife, but love covers all transgressions" (Proverbs 10:12).

Hot tempers: "A hot-tempered man stirs up strife, but the slow to anger calms a dispute" (Proverbs 15:18).

Slander: "A perverse man spreads strife, and a slanderer separates intimate friends" (Proverbs 16:28).

Rebellion: "He who loves transgression loves strife" (Proverbs 17:19).

Pride: "An arrogant man stirs up strife, but he who trusts in the LORD will prosper" (Proverbs 28:25).

Anger: "An angry man stirs up strife, and a hot-tempered man abounds in transgression" (Proverbs 29:22)

Take the Strife Out of Life

"Keeping away from strife is an honor for a man, but any fool will quarrel" (Proverbs 20:3). You will want to resolve your conflict because that is what pleases God. Jesus gave these instructions:

> "Therefore if you are presenting your offering at the altar, and there remember that your brother has something against you, leave your offering there before the altar and go; first be reconciled to your brother, and then come and present your offering."
>
> Matthew 5:23–24

The scribes and Pharisees taught that no act of worship should be interrupted, which meant they thought the offering was more important than the worshipper's heart. Jesus refuted their man-made rule by teaching that the worshipper's heart nullifies the offering if he or she harbors ill feelings toward another person. Jesus was talking about a brother who has something rightfully against you, not someone who is falsely accusing you of something you did not do. This rift in the relationship is something that you have done to hurt your brother, which requires that you try to resolve the issue.

Imagine a man taking his lamb to the temple to sacrifice as an act of worship. As he is about to hand his animal to the priest to place on the altar, a thought pops into his mind. The worshipper suddenly remembers a disagreement that he had with his enemy. His adversary stole some money from him, but he reacted poorly by calling him some hateful names. He realizes that he must forgive his enemy for wronging him, but he also needs to ask forgiveness for his hateful response.

Jesus tells him to leave his offering at the altar. There is nothing wrong with the offering, so there is no need to take it away. The offering is acceptable, but the worshipper's attitude is not, and God is looking at his heart. This passage reveals that the Lord is aware of what we are offering Him, what the attitude in our hearts is, and also the personal conflicts that we are experiencing.

The worshipper leaves his offering and walks three miles to where his enemy lives. He asks forgiveness for calling him those names and tells him that he forgives him for stealing from him. The enemy accepts his apology and they are reconciled, so he returns to the temple and presents his offering to God.

But suppose his enemy does not want to be reconciled. Instead of being receptive to him, his enemy curses him out and slams the door in his face. What is the worshipper to do? God accepts that fact that he did everything in his power to resolve the conflict. Perhaps his enemy will change his mind later and reconcile with him and God. The worshipper can now return to the altar with a clear conscience, knowing he did what Christ has asked of him.

Under the New Covenant, we do not take animals to the temple. The principle remains the same, however, when we give our tithes and offerings to the Lord. A wrong horizontal relationship with man will block our vertical relationship with God.

Sometimes we wonder why there is a barrier between God and us. We are puzzled that our prayers do not seem to be getting through. The reason may very well be that we have erected a barrier because we have wronged someone and have not made it right.

The Need for Forgiveness

Before you can resolve any conflict, you must first forgive the person who hurt you. Forgiveness is not reconciliation, but is the first step toward it, and is based on what Jesus did *for* you, not on what someone did *to* you. "Should you not also have had mercy on your fellow slave, in the same way that I had mercy on you?" (Matthew 18:33).

When you forgive, it does not mean that your enemies will suddenly love you. Jesus was perfect, yet He still had many enemies who hated Him. Nor does forgiveness mean that you put your stamp of approval on what the other person did. Forgiveness simply means to let go, which releases the anger from your heart. You know that you have forgiven someone when you stop tormenting yourself and you quit wishing harm on your opponent.

The cost of forgiveness is always borne by the one who does the forgiving. If I break your expensive vase and you forgive me, you suffer the loss and I go free. If I ruin your reputation and you forgive me, you bear the hurt and I go free. The amount you forgive is the amount you lose.

Once you forgive and let go, you are now free to move forward by taking steps to solve your disagreement.

How to Resolve Conflict

Not everyone reacts the same way when it comes to offense. Some people are Teflon—everything slides off and nothing sticks. Others are Velcro—nothing slides off and everything sticks, which means they are easily offended.

Proverbs 18:19 says, "A brother offended is harder to be won than a strong city, and contentions are like the bars of a citadel." In biblical times, a strong city was hard to defeat because of the walls surrounding it. People who have been offended put up walls around themselves as a defense mechanism. To be reconciled to this person, the walls must come down.

The cost of forgiveness is always borne by the one who does the forgiving.

Here are some steps to take to bring the walls down.

Step #1: You Must Make the First Move

When conflict occurs, we want to stand back and let the other person make the first move to resolve it. As time passes, nobody moves and the dispute gets worse as hearts harden.

God tells us to take the initiative and make the first move, which is why Jesus said to leave your offering at the altar and go to your offended brother first. Quit waiting for him to come to you.

The apostle Paul said, "Never pay back evil for evil to anyone. Respect what is right in the sight of all men. If possible, *so far as it depends on you*, be at peace with all men" (Romans 12:17–18, emphasis added). Notice the three parts of verse 18:

"If possible." This implies that the other person may not want to be reconciled. That individual may be dead set against even talking with you and has no intentions in being open to reconciliation. But it also means that resolving the conflict may be possible.

"So far as it depends on you." This puts the burden of peace-making on you. It will require humility on your part because your pride wants the other person to come to you. You must do everything within your power to resolve the problem. Quit waiting for the other person to make the first move. You must take the initiative and start the process.

"Be at peace with all men." Conflict creates friction, but reconciliation brings peace. These instructions apply to everyone, not just a few people. If you can live at peace with all people, you will have a peaceful life.

If you will make the first move, you will find that God will also make a move by blessing you. He will always bless the one who takes the initiative in peacemaking.

Some years ago, I noticed that a neighbor of mine seemed distant and did not want to communicate with me for some reason. Later I found out that someone who attended our church offended him while he was doing his duty as a city official.

Once I found this out, I immediately wrote him a letter apologizing for the treatment he had received and asked his forgiveness. I also told him that we believed government officials are servants of God and we intend to show the utmost respect to them.

As a result of this effort to make things right, he accepted our apology. Eventually we became good friends and he attended our church at times, even though he was a member of another denomination. Sometimes he would ask us to pray about various projects he was involved in. All this began when I first noticed he seemed offended and I made the first move to make it right.

God always blesses the one who takes the initiative in peacemaking.

Step #2: Do Not Delay in Taking Action

Jesus said:

> "*Make friends quickly* with your opponent at law while you are with him on the way, so that your opponent may not hand you over to the judge, and the judge to the officer, and you be thrown into prison. Truly I say to you, you will not come out of there until you have paid up the last cent."
>
> Matthew 5:25–26, emphasis added

He said to make friends with your opponent, and you must do it quickly. Do not delay! It is always easiest to put out a fire when it is small. You have a window of time to create a positive relationship with your enemy. Although this sounds impossible, Jesus would not have told us to do it if it could not be done. Perhaps if we would just obey His instructions, He would intervene and change the other person's heart.

Why should you do it? You will be headed for disastrous consequences if you do not. You would be wise to make every effort to resolve your differences by turning your opponent into a friend. Jesus says to do this "while you are with him on the way." On the way where? To court. The only time you have left is the journey to the courtroom. That does not give you much time; yet resolving the conflict is still possible.

How can you make friends quickly with someone who hates you? It begins with you apologizing for what you may have done wrong. Perhaps your opponent has believed incorrect information. You must do your best to clarify the situation with the truth. If the conflict was not intended, you need to make an appeal for mercy, saying something like, "I never intended to hurt you. Please forgive me."

> Who is the person that you hope is not living next door to you in heaven?

If you do not quickly make friends with your enemy, Jesus said that your opponent will turn you over to the judge, and the judge to the officer, and then you will be thrown in prison.

Although our justice system is different from back then, the principle is the same—put out the fire quickly and it will stop something worse from happening. "The beginning of strife is like letting out water, so abandon the quarrel before it breaks out" (Proverbs 17:14).

Step #3: Give a Gift to the Other Person

Who is the person that you hope is not living next door to you in heaven? That is your enemy. Jesus told us, "Love your enemies, do good to those who hate you, bless those who curse you, pray for those who mistreat you" (Luke 6:27–28).

One of the things God continues to teach me is, "Do not love reservedly, love fervently." First Peter 1:22 says to "fervently love one another from the heart." We do not use the word *fervently* very often, but the Greek word means "to stretch out." The idea here is that you are making every effort to reach out and love others, which includes giving gifts.

I have already talked about making deposits into others' accounts and given you some examples of how it has worked in my life. Perhaps the best biblical example is the case of Jacob and Esau. You will remember that when Jacob cheated Esau out of his birthright, Esau "bore a grudge" against him and planned to kill him after their father died (see Genesis 27:41). Jacob fled away, knowing he was not safe around Esau.

Years later, Jacob decided to reconcile with his brother. He sent messengers before him to arrange the meeting. Then Jacob gathered together hundreds of goats, along with rams, camels, cows, bulls and donkeys as gifts for Esau. He sent his servants with the animals ahead of him in groups, with a distance between each group. Jacob understood the impact it would make if he showered Esau with multiple blessings.

As Esau met each servant with their gifts, they said, "These belong to your servant Jacob; it is a present sent to my lord Esau. And behold, he also is behind us" (Genesis 32:18). Jacob sent gifts to Esau in waves, and you can almost visualize Esau's hard, bitter heart melting as he received each gift. By the time they met, "Esau ran to meet him and embraced him, and fell on his neck and kissed him, and they wept" (Genesis 33:4).

Jacob's strategy worked because reconciliation with Esau was more important to him than keeping those animals for himself. Jacob was willing to give away his property to resolve the dispute with Esau. He made a good trade, realizing that you cannot put a price tag on having peace of mind.

Presenting your enemy with a gift will go a long way in resolving your conflict. Think about what your enemy would like to receive, and then go get that item as a gift. If you are willing to bless your adversary in some way, God will be pleased and will bless you for doing it.

Step #4: Find Common Ground

Have you ever considered that common ground can make people forget their differences? You will find liberal Democrats and conservative Republicans hugging each other and giving high fives—if they are pulling for the same football team that scores a touchdown! During football season, millions of people with opposing political views are seated together in stadiums, pulling for the same team. As long as they are focused on a common interest, they are not thinking about their differences.

SECRET #4

Make the first move and surprise your enemy with a gift.

This principle is also true in finding common ground with your foe. If you and your spouse are in conflict, it is because you are magnifying your differences. If you think about it, however, you have many things in common. If you are both Christians, you have your relationship with the Lord in common.

"Draw near to God and He will draw near to you" (James 4:8). The way to get a piano in tune is by using a tuning fork. When a husband and wife both get in tune with God, they will be in tune with each other. Their unity with the Lord will make their differences seem minor.

What mutual ground do you have with the person you have a conflict with? In what ways can you magnify the things you have in common? Finding areas of agreement is vital in smoothing out your differences.

Step #5: Communicate in a Non-Threatening Way

The way you communicate with your opponent will either make matters better or worse. Proverbs 15:1 says, "A gentle answer turns away wrath, but a harsh word stirs up anger."

Notice that it is not the words that create the different responses, but the tone of voice and the manner in which the words are delivered. You can soften a person's heart by speaking words of kindness, not rude words. "Not returning evil for evil or *insult for insult, but giving a blessing instead*; for you were called for the very purpose that you might inherit a blessing" (1 Peter 3:9, emphasis added).

Have you ever had an imaginary argument with someone who is at odds with you? You are preparing yourself for the next time you meet the person. "I will say this, then she will say this, and I will respond by saying this. . . ." This angry conversation inside your mind will almost certainly make the relationship worse with your opponent.

First, you are making an assumption about what the other person will say without giving him or her a chance. Second, you are programming yourself to react negatively based on your presumptions. An imaginary argument can become a self-fulfilling prophecy. God's Word tells us to cast down those vain imaginations (see 2 Corinthians 10:5).

Instead of having an angry conversation in your mind, see yourself speaking kindly and calmly to the individual. Program yourself to win their friendship. As you gently talk with your opponent, express your desire to correct any wrong that you were responsible for doing. Then listen to what the other person has to say, without cutting him or her off. Seek to understand what the other person has against you. Never put the full blame on them. Admit your part in doing wrong.

Avoid using the words "never" and "always." Do not attack each other in the discussion. Agree to be open to all topics related to your disagreement. Encourage the person to express how he or she feels. If there is misunderstanding, you will need to clarify the issues.

Whenever I hear someone is upset at me, I immediately apologize for offending him or her. A good thing to say is, "Please tell me what I did to offend you, and what I need to do to make it right as far as you are concerned." Usually this will open up communication and they will start to respond.

Keep the door open and let them know that you want to settle accounts. Never close the door to possible reconciliation. In some cases, you may need to use a referee. Get help from a neutral person outside of your relationship, such as a counselor. This person can help you work through your differences and interpret what each one is saying.

The highest form of communication is praying together because it reaches out to God in the spiritual realm. If the other person is open to praying together, seize the opportunity. It may create a huge breakthrough. If the other person is not open to this, however, do not force the issue.

I knew a man who was very angry at churches because he had been hurt at one in another city. He knew I was a pastor, but this did not deter him from spewing his venom. Whenever he would talk with me, he would always get around to bad-mouthing every church in town.

I was tempted to run whenever I saw him coming because no one likes to be hated and criticized. But I knew I needed to keep listening if I was going to reach him. I knew I could never help him if I turned my back on him.

One day I found out he was sick. My wife said to me, "I know he is a mean man and no one likes to be around him, but I think we need to go visit him in his home and pray for him." I agreed.

When we entered his house, he was lying on the couch. Instead of being glad we were there, he immediately started his bitter rant about churches. After he finished, I tried to communicate with him in a compassionate way.

I asked him, "Have you noticed how angry you are? Don't you see how it is destroying you? Wouldn't you like to have some peace in your life? The only way you'll find it is by accepting Jesus Christ into your life."

He broke down and admitted he was not a happy person. I prayed with him and led him to faith in Jesus that day. When he died, I conducted his funeral. But if I had not made an effort to reach him when he was pushing me away, he might not be in heaven right now.

Step #6: Compromise Where You Can

Compromise minimizes your differences. Compromising does not mean that you give up your convictions about God, but that you lay down your "right" to be "right." It means you sit down with the other person and negotiate your differences so you can come to an agreement.

Philippians 2:4 says, "Do not merely look out for your own personal interests, but also for the interests of others." Compromising means you meet halfway to settle your differences. Both parties give a little so that they can get along rather than constantly fight over the same issues.

I know a married couple who used to argue about what temperature to set the thermostat in their house. In the summertime, the husband liked it warm but the wife wanted it to snow inside. They came to an agreement to set the temperature in between, where they both had to give a little.

This couple negotiated with each other and compromised hundreds of times over the years, where they both had to give in a little bit. As a result, they rarely argued and have a wonderful marriage.

> **Compromising means you lay down your "right" to be "right."**

The husband also told me how they went about making important decisions. They prayed God would bring them into agreement when it was the right thing to do. If one of them did not feel right, it meant that either the timing was wrong, or God was using one spouse's uneasiness to keep them from making a mistake.

If you will put these six steps into practice, you will be able to resolve most conflicts. And if the other person does not want to make peace, at least you have done your part. Leave the rest in God's hands.

Discussion Questions

Pursuing Peacemaking

What are some reasons people have conflict?

Read Matthew 5:23–24. Why does God tell you to not give any offerings to Him until you make an attempt to reconcile with someone?

Discuss this statement: "Forgiveness means to release the anger out of your heart."

Romans 12:18 says, "If possible, so far as it depends on you, be at peace with all men." What does it mean to "make the first move" when it comes to reconciliation?

Read Matthew 5:25. Why is it important to "make friends quickly" with someone who threatens to sue you?

Esau hated Jacob and threatened to kill him. What happened to Esau's heart when Jacob showered him with gifts? How can we apply this to our own strained relationships?

Read Proverbs 15:1. How can your tone of voice either provoke anger or extinguish it?

Challenge #5

HEALING YOUR HURTS

A person with a toothache cannot fall in love.

—Freud

As a longtime pastor, I have been on the receiving end of more attacks and criticisms than I care to remember. Church members have falsely accused me of things that simply were not true, and it hurt deeply. If I had taken all their criticisms to heart, I probably would have left the ministry. I realize that most pastors are frequently criticized because of Satan's spiritual attacks.

When you have been hurt, it is tempting to get revenge in one way or another. Sometimes I wanted to just run away from people, and at other times I wanted to kill them! Of course, neither was the correct way to respond.

I know you can identify with my feelings. You cannot walk through life without getting hurt by someone, which is your fifth challenge. Maybe you have been rejected, abandoned, or physically abused. Perhaps someone said hateful words to you many years ago, but you can still hear them in your mind today. How you handle your hurts will determine if you skip through life with a smile or limp through life while licking your wounds.

King David said, "For I am afflicted and needy, and my heart is wounded within me" (Psalm 109:22). David confessed that his heart had been wounded. He was not talking about an injury to his physical heart but to his soul.

Do you understand how a wounded spirit can affect your relationships? It programs or conditions you to respond to others in unhealthy ways. When two separate experiences are linked together, they will produce a similar response.

Suppose you move into a new apartment and get into the shower. After washing for a few minutes with warm water, you hear the pipes rattle, which is then followed by a burst of cold water. When the cold water hits you, you jump back, and a few seconds later the water turns warm again. The tenant in the apartment below turned on her shower, which diverted the hot water to her instead of you.

Over the next few days, the same thing happens every time you take a shower. The pipes rattle, which is followed by cold water. By now you have learned to get out of the way when the pipes rattle because you know cold water is coming next.

The rattling of the pipes has *conditioned you* to jump back. Now you are not responding to the cold water hitting

> How you handle your hurts will determine whether you skip through life with a smile or limp through life while licking your wounds.

you, but to the noise that precedes it. The cold water and the noisy pipes have been associated together in your mind, so now you are reacting to the sound just as you would the icy water.

Step 1:   Cold water = jump
Step 2:   Rattling + cold water = jump
Step 3:   Rattling = jump

This explains why you crave popcorn when you go to the movies. You have eaten popcorn so many times while you have watched movies that popcorn munching and movie watching have been connected together. Now you cannot watch a movie without eating popcorn—and you will even pay outrageous prices to get it!

What does this have to do with inner wounds? Everything.

When someone hurts you, the conditioning process begins. If you do not forgive the individual and move on with your life, your pain will cause you to react to others in the same way as the person who hurt you.

If someone reminds you of the person who hurt you, the "pipes rattle" and you jump back. If a person says similar words that you heard from someone who abused you, the bell rings and you put up your guard. You have been conditioned to react out of your hurt, and it will make you afraid of forming relationships for fear of being wounded again.

If you have been burned by a bad experience in a church, you may avoid all churches because you assume that the incident will be repeated. You have been conditioned to associate church with pain. If you had an abusive father who beat you, you may be conditioned to think that any man who looks like your dad will beat you too.

An unhealed wound creates a distorted lens through which you view others, and this causes you to overreact and become emotional. You are responding to what you *perceive* to be occurring rather than what is actually happening. Only God can heal your emotions, which will correct your perspective and bring your emotions back into normality.

Different Kinds of Wounds

Hurts can come from your friends or enemies, or you may have caused your own injury. Sores on your soul can come from the mistakes you make, the betrayals you experience, or hurtful memories you cling to. These wounds are usually delivered in four different ways.

Self-Inflicted Wounds

Sometimes we suffer as a result of the consequences of our own poor choices. These consequences are called self-inflicted wounds. Scripture says, "Make sure that none of you suffers as a murderer, or thief, or evildoer, or a troublesome meddler" (1 Peter 4:15). When we choose to sin in these ways, we will eventually pay the price in some way.

In the 1930s, boxer C. D. Blalock threw an incredible knockout punch. In one of the strangest moments in the history of boxing, Blalock took a swing at his opponent, missed, and hit himself in the face. He momentarily staggered around the ring and then fell down for the count. Blalock became the only professional boxer in history to ever score a knockout against himself.

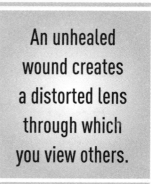

An unhealed wound creates a distorted lens through which you view others.

Sometimes we knock ourselves out or shoot ourselves in the foot by making foolish choices. We have no one to blame but ourselves for these wounds. Self-inflicted wounds are usually manifested through feelings of *guilt* and *regret*.

Battle Scars

These are wounds received while fighting with someone. You would be wise to carefully choose your battles and avoid the rest. God does not call you to fight in every war. Josiah was a good king, but he got involved in a battle God never wanted him to fight and died as a result (see 2 Chronicles 35:20–24).

Far too many people are wounded because they stick their nose where it should not be. They are fighting wars they should not be fighting. When someone tries to pick a fight, it may take more courage to ignore the challenge and walk away.

An antagonistic person takes a jab at you and tries to start an argument. Jesus told you to turn the other cheek and not take the bait, but you choose to ignore God's wisdom and retaliate anyway. You are fighting evil with evil rather than overcoming evil with good. That is engaging in a battle you should not be fighting, and internal injuries are often the result. Battle scars may be manifested through feelings of *anger* and *revenge*.

Friendly Fire

These wounds are caused by a friend or loved one, which usually involves being betrayed by someone you have trusted or rejected by someone you have loved. "Friendly fire" is a military term used when soldiers are wounded or killed by someone from their own side, either accidentally or intentionally. These kinds of casualties occur more often than many people realize.

Stonewall Jackson, a well-known Confederate general, was killed in 1863 by his own troops. A military historian claims that probably 10 percent of nearly a million American World War II casualties were the result of friendly fire. The Vietnam War records between 15 and 20 percent of American casualties were a result of friendly fire.[1]

I know a man who was faithfully serving in Christian ministry when a friend whom he had trusted betrayed him. The person who hurt him had done something unethical and clearly was in the wrong. Even though the minister took the correct side of the issue, he allowed himself to get offended, and bitterness grew in his heart. He refused to forgive the man and would not let go of his hurt.

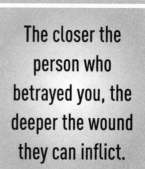

The closer the person who betrayed you, the deeper the wound they can inflict.

His unwillingness to forgive eventually destroyed him. His bitterness spread into his spiritual life and also to his marriage. He turned his back on God and dropped out of the ministry. His marriage ended in a nasty divorce. All this occurred because he would not let God heal his wounded spirit.

Friendly fire can come from a fellow church member or a next-door neighbor. Family feuds can cause injuries to your soul as well. A divorce probably causes the deepest wound because the person who vowed to love you until death turned against you. Generally speaking, the closer the person who betrayed you, the deeper the wound they can inflict.

David also received some wounds from friendly fire. He said, "Even my close friend in whom I trusted, who ate my

1. David M. Foster, "Wounded by 'Friendly Fire,'" *Light and Life*, July 2, 1994.

bread, has lifted up his heel against me" (Psalm 41:9). Again he said:

> For it is not an enemy who reproaches me, then I could bear it; nor is it one who hates me who has exalted himself against me, then I could hide myself from him. But it is you, a man my equal, my companion and my familiar friend. We who had sweet fellowship together, walked in the house of God in the throng.
>
> Psalm 55:12–14

David's experience can also happen to us. Those closest to us, those whom we thought were our friends, often betray us. These wounds can be manifested through feelings of *rejection* and *bitterness*.

Innocent Victims

Some wounds come through no fault of your own, but through what others have done to you. Maybe someone molested or abused you as a child and you are still having nightmares about it. Perhaps a parent rejected you and it hurts every time you think about it. A teacher belittled you or called you a derogatory name, and you still carry that wound. Your classmates made fun of the way you looked or acted, and that made you feel inferior. You are an innocent victim of someone else's cruelty. These wounds are often manifested through feelings of *inadequacy* and *shame*.

These four areas describe general ways people can become wounded in their souls. You cannot slap a Band-Aid on them and hope they will go away. Inner wounds are different from physical injuries. If you do not get emotionally healed, your hurts can turn to hate.

The good news is God can heal your hurts from the past, but how do you know if you still need to be healed? Here are five signs that indicate you are still aching from past hurts.

Signs of a Wounded Spirit

Symptom #1: If You Are Easily Offended and Hurt

People with wounded spirits have a very low tolerance for pain, which makes them hypersensitive in their area of hurt. As a result, it is easy for them to be reinjured.

When an innocent remark that would not bother a healthy person offends someone, it usually means that individual is nursing an unhealed wound. The incident that hurt them so badly may have happened years ago, but they are still aching today. It is buried deep inside and the similarity to a previous tragedy triggers a conditioned response.

If you push their "hurt" button, they will respond by lashing out at you. They are actually reacting to the original wounding, and you innocently did something that reminded them of it.

Suppose that every time your friend is around, he hits you on the same place on your arm. At first it does not bother you, but he keeps doing it. Every time he punches you, it hurts a little more. You ask him to stop doing it, but he will not. He keeps hitting you on the exact same spot until you finally develop a bruise. You are now hypersensitive in that area because of your sore spot.

If someone touches you on your other arm, it will not hurt. But if someone lightly touches your wounded arm, you will flinch in pain because you are extremely susceptible in that area.

Now suppose that someone comes up to you and accidentally bumps into your sore spot. You go reeling in pain—not because of what that person did, but because of what your friend did to hurt you before. The person who bumped into you does not understand why you are reacting in that way.

You can grasp the concept of a sore spot on your physical body, but the same reality applies to your spirit. Wounded people are hypersensitive in their area of hurt. All someone has to do is push the sore spot. If you make an innocent comment to a wounded person, it triggers a hurtful memory. The injured person overreacts because he or she has been conditioned to respond to something that happened years before.

This explains why the divorce rate goes up with every successive remarriage. The sore spots keep multiplying. When conflict occurs in the remarriage, the new spouse creates new sore spots, which add to the sore spots the spouse received in the first marriage. A third marriage adds even more soreness to a person who is already suffering from two previous marriages.

Can you now see why it is so important to get healed inside? If you do not, you will keep overreacting because you have been conditioned to respond in this way. The slightest pressure on a sore spot can unleash all the pent-up anger and hostility buried inside a person. It does not matter how many years ago the incident occurred, the sensitivity remains the same, as if the offense happened yesterday.

Symptom #2: If You Keep Talking About and Thinking About Your Hurt

Wounded people will continually talk about how someone hurt them. They keep "visiting" the event that caused the wound by replaying the hurt in their minds. And every time they hit the "play" button, they watch the offense take place again and get wounded one more time.

When you are first injured, you do need to talk about it. If you have been hurt, you will need to vent. Part of the healing process is to sort through your feelings. But a time comes when it has to stop. You must forgive, let go, and get on with your life. People who choose not to get over something will keep talking about it, sometimes for years. They will never get healed until they decide to let go.

Symptom #3: If You Are Overly Suspicious of Others

A person with a wounded spirit will view others suspiciously because he or she thinks everyone is out to hurt them. King Saul imagined that David was trying to steal his throne, which was not true. Because he felt endangered, "Saul looked at David with suspicion from that day on" (1 Samuel 18:9). Even though David was innocent, Saul became overly suspicious of his intentions.

Suppose a pet owner continually beat his dog, Spot, with a stick. One day Spot walks down the street and a boy picks up a stick to play fetch with it. When the dog sees him pick up the stick, it takes off running with its tail between its legs. See Spot run.

Why did the dog run away? The dog had been *conditioned* to associate the stick with being beaten. The abuse it received as a puppy programmed the dog to assume that anyone holding a stick would attack. The boy wanted to innocently play with it, but the dog misinterpreted his motives due to its painful past.

Can you see how wounded people react the same way? After someone has beaten you up, you may start viewing everyone with suspicion. If you assume they have a hidden agenda to hurt you, you will react by pulling away from them.

Jill was continually accusing her husband, Rick, of being overly interested in other women. When she was a girl, her father left her mother for another woman and abandoned her family. Because of this devastating past hurt, Jill was terrified that Rick would do the same thing to her. Her false accusations were slowly killing their marriage.

Rick loved her and had no intentions of abandoning her. Yet because of the wounding she received as a child, Jill became unrealistically suspicious. Each false accusation pushed him a little further away.

Fortunately, a counselor helped her realize her past wound was the source of her insecurity and not her husband. If she had not realized this, she may very well have destroyed her marriage.

Symptom #4: If It Is Hard for You to Love Others

An individual who is hurting inside has a difficult time loving others because he is consumed with his own pain. All his attention goes to his own hurt, so that makes it extremely hard to concentrate on other people's needs.

If a soldier is wounded in battle, it is nearly impossible for him to have the motivation to help another wounded soldier. His own anguish short-circuits his concern for others. A hero might make an effort to help someone else in the same condition, but an injured soldier's greatest need is to get to a hospital to get well. After his wound is healed, he is then able to care for others.

The same is true for someone nursing inner wounds. The first priority is to get healthy, which then frees a person to reach out to those in need.

Symptom #5: If You Keep Others at a Distance

Wounded people do not want to get hurt again, so they often keep others at a distance. Proverbs 18:19 says, "A brother offended is harder to be won than a strong city, and contentions are like the bars of a citadel." In biblical times, a strong city had fortified walls, which were constructed to defend the inhabitants. This made the city difficult to capture. People who have been offended are hard to befriend because they have constructed invisible walls around themselves to keep others from getting too close.

A man who had been jilted by a girlfriend kept telling his male friends, "Never trust a woman." Without realizing it, he had constructed a wall of self-defense around himself to keep his former girlfriend away. He made the wall so big it kept every woman on the planet out of his life as well.

Why would he say such a thing? Obviously, it is not true that no woman on earth could be trusted. He made that comment because he had been wounded deeply and did not want to take a chance on being hurt again. That is the wrong solution to the problem. The correct remedy is to ask God to heal your wounds.

Let God Heal You

Suppose you were raised in an environment where others treated you as inferior. Perhaps it was because of your race, physical appearance, intelligence or some other factor. Whatever the reason, you did not measure up to your peers' expectations. Because they viewed you as inferior, they treated you as unimportant and insignificant. Their derogatory words and rejection programmed you to think of yourself as really inferior to others. And it hurts.

Now, suppose you receive Christ into your life. He instantly comes to dwell in you and gives you a new nature. The Spirit that raised Him from the dead now dwells inside you!

But if the Spirit of Him who raised Jesus from the dead dwells in you, He who raised Christ Jesus from the dead will also give life to your mortal bodies through His Spirit who dwells in you.

Romans 8:11

Receiving the new nature changes everything, including the way you think. "But we have the mind of Christ" (1 Corinthians 2:16). When you renew your mind, you learn to process with "God thoughts." In other words, you see yourself as the Lord sees you. You view your hurtful situation from His perspective.

Soon you discover that no one is inferior in His sight and He loves all people equally. Once you exchange the lie you once believed for the truth of God's Word, it will set you free. Jesus said, "And you will know the truth, and the truth will make you free" (John 8:32).

This mind-change is an important key to being healed of your hurts. You must see those who wounded you in a new light, and not see yourself as a victim anymore. Here are a few important ingredients in finding complete freedom from the past.

1. Desperately Seek God to Be Healed

Jesus was at the pool of Bethesda when He saw a man who had been unable to walk for 38 years. He looked at him and asked the strangest question, "Do you wish to get well?" (John 5:6). The man had not walked for almost four decades and Jesus asked if he wanted to be healed! Some people might have thought that question was insensitive.

The answer seems like a no-brainer. You would think everyone would say yes.

But Jesus never wasted His words. This question prompted the man to examine his own heart, so he would ask himself, *Do I really want to walk? If He heals me, it will change the way I do things. Other people have carried me around and I am used to that. If I am healed, I will have to take responsibility for myself. Do I want that?*

It is a question that all wounded people must answer. "Do I really want to get well?"

Many people who have wounded spirits do not want to get over their hurts. They prefer to stay bitter and angry. If you truly want to get past your past you must desperately ask God to heal you. If you are not serious about this, you probably will not receive freedom from the past incident. A necessary key to receiving healing is desperation on your part.

Jesus was traveling through Jericho when a blind beggar named Bartimaeus cried out, "Jesus, Son of David, have mercy on me!" (Mark 10:47). Bartimaeus was so desperate that he did not care the crowd was telling him to shut up. The man's urgent cry for mercy caught Jesus' attention, but He wanted him to be more specific in his appeal.

Again, Jesus looked at the blind man and asked a ridiculous question, which seemed to have an obvious answer. "What do you want me to do for you?"

Bartimaeus could have said, "I would like a seeing-eye dog" or "How about giving me a white cane?" It is easy for us to settle for less than what God wants to do for us.

The blind man blurted out, "I want to regain my sight!"

Of course, his request was impossible, humanly speaking. They did not have eye surgeons like we have today, and although many miracles were recorded in the Old Testament, there is no mention of a blind person ever being healed. Even the Pharisees admitted, "Since the beginning of time it has never been heard that anyone opened the eyes of a person born blind" (John 9:32). Bartimaeus had never seen Jesus but trusted Him enough to ask for a miracle—and he got it!

It might not have happened if he hadn't called out to Him in sheer desperation.

If Jesus could heal a blind man by just speaking to him, don't you think He can do a miracle for you and heal your inner wounds? Yes, He can.

He asks the same question of you, when you cry out for healing from your past hurts. "What do you want Me to do for you?"

Examine yourself and be honest. Do you really want to be made well?

2. Genuinely Forgive the Person Who Hurt You

Many people are still hurting from something that happened five, ten, or fifteen years ago. If time could heal wounds, that should be long enough to do it. So if time does not heal hurts, what does?

Forgiveness heals. You must forgive everyone who hurt you of everything they have done. Unforgiveness is one of the main reasons people are not healed of their wounds. Forgiving the person who hurt you will set you free.

You are handcuffed to the person that you do not forgive. You take the unforgiven person with you wherever you go. When you go to bed at night, the invisible person is there to keep you awake. When you go on a vacation, the unforgiven person travels with you to your destination, ruining your trip. You cannot get away from your enemy because you have chosen to stay attached through your unwillingness to forgive. And here is a scary thought—you will take that person with you to your grave unless you unlock the handcuffs.

As Stephen was being stoned, although he committed no crime, his last words were, "Lord, do not hold this sin against them!" (Acts 7:60). Even as they were killing him,

Stephen knew the importance of being an instant forgiver. He would be standing before God a few minutes later and did not want to have unforgiveness on his record.

Years ago, I was counseling with a married couple. In the middle of our session, the wife confessed to her husband that she had an affair with another man. Her husband was caught totally off guard by her admission, as he had no idea that she had betrayed him. As you can imagine, it devastated him to hear this. He broke down and started weeping uncontrollably. It was as if she had taken a knife and stabbed him in his heart. At the time, it looked like there was no possible way for this marriage to survive.

You know that you have forgiven when you stop wishing evil to come on those who have hurt you.

After much prayer, however, the husband decided to forgive his wife for her infidelity. He chose to move forward with the marriage instead of filing for divorce. This happened nearly forty years ago and they are now in retirement. Having known this couple for all those years, I can honestly tell you that they have been happily married since then, and it is all because he genuinely forgave her.

The key to forgiving others is to realize how much the Lord has forgiven us. God says, "I will remember their sins no more" (Hebrews 8:12), which means He chooses to not hold our sin against us. He does not keep bringing it up, and if we have forgiven someone, we will not continue bringing it up either.

Forgiveness opens the way to receive healing. Stop wishing evil to come on those who have hurt you. You must release the anger out of your heart so that you are not upset anymore. Have you done this?

3. Let Go of the Painful Incident

Someone has said, "You cannot pray with a clenched fist." As long as you are holding on to your hurt, you will never be able to release it through prayer. It will control your emotions. If your pain tells you to get angry, you will get angry. If it tells you to pout and feel sorry for yourself, you will do that too. But if you let go of it, it cannot tell you what to do anymore.

You can hold on to things with your hands, but you can also hold on to things with your heart. "Letting go" means releasing what you are holding on to in your spirit. How do you let go of an object in your hand? Your mind tells your fingers to release it and your hand obeys. To let go of inner hurts, your mind tells your heart to "let go" of the person or incident by an act of your will.

"Letting go" means . . .

- You will let God take care of your situation instead of you.
- You cannot control another person's attitudes and actions, so you will not try.
- You will not let your past determine your future.
- You will not let your past condemn you, but you will learn from it.
- You do not deny what happened to you, but you will admit it and forgive.
- You will not allow domineering people to manipulate or take advantage of you anymore.
- You will not take your own revenge, but will leave vengeance to God.

You can let go of your bad memories by not replaying the incident in your mind. You let go of people by releasing them into God's hands. Just as God spoke through Moses to Pharaoh, "Let My people go," God is giving the same command to you: "Let him go. Let her go."

SECRET #5

Forgiving others and letting go opens the door for your complete healing.

Imagine placing the person who hurt you into your cupped hands. You come before the Lord with your hands cupped and place your hands inside His hands. Then you gently move your hands apart, leaving the person in God's hands. You now have closure.

After you let go, you can now move on with your life. No more limping through life, licking your wounds—only a clean slate and a new future. Now you can skip through life with a smile on your face!

Discussion Questions

Receiving Healing

Discuss how a person becomes "conditioned" to react in a certain way.

What are some ways that we inflict wounds on ourselves?

Have you ever been betrayed by someone? How did you deal with it?

What does the story about the dog that was beaten with a stick teach you about the way wounded people view others?

Read Proverbs 18:19. Why is an offended person hard to win back?

Read John 5:2–9 and Mark 10:46–52. Why is desperation an important part in receiving healing from God?

What did you learn from Stephen about forgiving those who hurt you? (Acts 7:52–60)

What does it mean to "let go"? How can you symbolically let go of someone?

ADJUSTING YOUR ATTITUDES

Ability is what you're capable of doing. Attitude determines how well you do it.

—Raymond Chandler

Your sixth challenge involves improving your attitude, which will bring about a change in your behavior and how you view your circumstances.

It is hard to act like a Christian if you are not a Christian. Imagine a horse getting up every day saying, "I've got to act like a cow today if I am going to get to heaven. I can't 'neigh' anymore; I've got to 'moo.' I can't get up on my front legs first, but I must stand up like a cow, on my back legs first." But if I could get a needle and somehow inject "cow life" into a horse, the horse would begin to act like a cow.

The Lord has injected "God life" into every believer so that we can live like Him. The only way we can manifest the proper attitudes is by getting them from God. Attitude is your positive or negative evaluation of people, objects, ideas and circumstances. Everyone has an attitude, but most people do not understand the extraordinary power it has to make their lives much better or much worse.

> There is little difference in people, but that little difference makes a big difference! The little difference is attitude. The big difference is whether it is positive or negative.
>
> W. Clement Stone[1]

Your attitude will determine your altitude. In the game of football, some players are called "difference makers." They are so extremely skilled that they can make the difference between winning and losing. But if the player has a bad attitude and creates strife with his teammates, he will do more harm than good.

You have one of those gifted players on your team right now. It is called attitude. Your attitude is your *difference maker* that can turn around everything in your life, but it depends on how you use it. Attitude will make the difference between:

. . . a happy marriage or an ugly divorce.

. . . being promoted or fired.

. . . feeling elation or depression.

. . . experiencing success or failure.

Toxic Attitudes

In the 1970s, a chemical company buried 21,000 tons of toxic waste in the Love Canal area near Niagara Falls. Not long

---

1. Napoleon Hill and W. Clement Stone, *Success Through a Positive Mental Attitude* (Englewood Cliffs, N.J.: Prentice-Hall, 1960; New York: Pocket Books, 2007), 279. Citation refers to the Pocket Books edition.

after covering up the problem, the toxic waste seeped into the groundwater and then to the surface. Vegetation in the neighborhood started dying and an unusually high number of people reported having cancer, miscarriages and other medical problems.

Some people try to cover up their toxic attitudes, but they will eventually surface and contaminate everyone in the neighborhood. Bad attitudes can infect the heart just as chemicals can poison the body. I have discussed unforgiveness and rebellion in other chapters, but here are some more toxic attitudes:

Pessimism

A little boy snuck into the bedroom of his grandfather when he was sleeping. He stuck some Limburger cheese on his mustache and then slipped out of the room. A little while later, the grandfather woke sniffing.

"This bedroom stinks," he muttered.

He walked into the next room and said, "This living room stinks."

As he entered the kitchen, he snapped, "This kitchen stinks, too!"

Finally he walked outside, took a whiff, and yelled, "The whole world stinks!"

Some people have Limburger cheese in their attitudes. Wherever they go, it stinks. But the problem really is not the people or circumstances, but their own stinking attitude.

Pessimism is having a stinking attitude toward your circumstances. Pessimists have programmed themselves to look for what is wrong in every situation, which always produces complaints and criticisms. They will complain about circumstances because they have lost their appreciation for life, and they will criticize people because they have lost their compassion for others.

As compassion decreases, criticism increases. As compassion increases, criticism deceases. If you do not view others with love, you will only see their faults.

The sad truth is that a negative attitude works like a reverse "Midas touch." It turns everything it touches into a muffler. A pessimist will never become an optimist unless there is a radical change of heart. Until the heart changes, nothing changes.

Anger

A man was driving on a Philadelphia expressway when the traffic stopped. Cars had backed up and were being funneled into a single lane. The man became angry and upset because he was late for an appointment.

Just as he was about to pull into the lane, he noticed a car behind him driving on the shoulder, speeding past all the stalled cars. The car came off the shoulder and cut in front of him, which pushed his hot button. He laid on his horn to let the other driver know what he thought of his stunt. The driver of the car that cut in front turned around and made an obscene gesture at him.

Now the man was fuming. He grabbed his pistol out of the glove compartment, walked up to the car in front of him, and killed the driver.

What angers you controls you. Most murders start with anger that gets out of control. Marriages die for the same reason. E. Stanley Jones, the missionary to India, once said, "Action has killed its thousands, but reaction its ten thousands." Anger is our hostile reaction to people and circumstances we do not like.

We get angry when others do something we do not want them to do, or when they are not doing something we want them to do. We have expectations that are not being met.

A father tells his daughter to clean her room. Later that day, he sees the room has not been cleaned. He gets mad because she did not do what he wanted, so he grounds her for the weekend. Now the daughter is mad at her dad because he did something she did not want him to do.

Anger becomes toxic when we get upset too frequently, even about small things. It is not a sin to be angry, but it becomes sinful if we hold on to it too long. The Scripture tells us, "Be angry, and yet do not sin; do not let the sun go down on your anger, and do not give the devil an opportunity" (Ephesians 4:26–27). Anger that is two days old opens the door to more toxic attitudes—jealousy, revenge and bitterness. For this reason, God says to resolve your anger quickly.

> **We get angry when others do something we do not want, or when they are not doing something we do want.**

How can anger be controlled? It begins by lowering your expectations of others. If you become angry because someone does not meet your expectations, the problem might be that you have placed the bar too high.

It is easy to be a perfectionist, expecting everyone else to act perfectly so that we can be happy. Of course, no one is perfect, and when the bar is set so high that no one can reach it, we will always be upset and angry over the performances of others. We fail to realize the problem really is not in their performance but with our unrealistic expectations.

A person with a servant's heart rarely gets upset at others. "For the anger of man does not achieve the righteousness of God" (James 1:20). Stop getting angry over the things you cannot change. Accept the fact that life is not fair. Play the cards that are dealt to you and leave the results in God's hands.

Worry

"Fear not" is one of the greatest commandments in the Bible. It is repeated so many times in Scripture because our natural tendency is to fear. Worry is fear of the future. We do not worry about things that have already happened. We are afraid of things that might happen in the future. We think, *What if I lose my job? What if terrorists strike? What if someone breaks into my house?* And the worry list never ends.

One night a married couple heard a noise in their house in the middle of the night. The husband went downstairs to investigate and found a burglar putting their silverware in a bag. He told the burglar, "Wait right here. I want to go get my wife. She has been expecting you every night for the last twenty years."

When we worry, we exchange a good night's sleep for tossing and turning in torment. It is not a good trade. But when we learn to trust God, He makes this promise: "When you lie down, you will not be afraid. When you lie down, your sleep will be sweet" (Proverbs 3:24).

Most of the things we worry about will never occur. A study revealed that 92 percent of the things we worry about are not going to happen. You are probably saying, "Yeah, but it is the other eight percent that I'm worried about! What about those things?"

The other 8 percent will not be as bad as you think, or God will give you the grace to get through it. Once you fully grasp that truth, you will have no reason to worry. Learn to live one day at a time and do not try to tackle any problem prematurely.

A man and wife were driving to see some friends and remembered that they had to drive over an old, rickety bridge. The wife said, "What are we going to do when we get to the bridge? We can't drive over it because it is unsafe."

"There's no other way to get across the river," the husband replied.

"But what if it collapses and we drown? Who will take care of our children?"

For the next hour, they talked and fretted about crossing the rickety old bridge. When they arrived at the river, they found out that a new bridge had been built to get across. They had worried about a problem that did not exist and lost an hour of joy as a result.

How many times have you worried about the rickety bridge? Do not lose any more of your joy through worrying. Cross each bridge when you come to it and not before. God already knows ahead of time where you are going, and if you have surrendered your life to Him, your future is in His hands. He will take care of the future bridges you will need to cross.

Worrying is more stressful on us than actually going through what we fear. God will give you His peace and grace to get through all of life's challenges. Trust God to be in control of your future. Remember that worry never trusts—and trust never worries. If you are afraid of tomorrow, it is because you are not trusting God to be in control and to take care of you.

That does not mean bad things will not happen. The disciples asked Jesus about the signs of His Second Coming. He told them, "And you will be hearing of wars and rumors of wars. *See that you are not frightened*" (Matthew 24:6, emphasis added).

Jesus picked a worst-case scenario and, even in that situation, told us to not be afraid. Wars and rumors of wars can be frightening if we do not believe He is in control. But the very fact that He predicted the future means that God is still in charge, even when nations are battling each other. He could not prophesy about the future unless He was in control of those events—and He specifically told His followers not to worry when it happens.

His command to not be afraid also means that He is watching over each one of us. He would not tell you that unless He was present to protect and provide for you. The next time you are tempted to be fearful of the future, remember this verse and tell God, "Lord, You told me not to be afraid, and I am going to trust You." Trusting God is the only way to conquer worry.

Healthy Attitudes

Your mind is like a television set. If you do not like what you see, you need to change channels. Turn off the toxic channel and tune in to the Healthy Mind Network.

When your mind gets cluttered with the wrong information, you will get stressed out and worried. You cannot choose what will happen to you, but you can choose your attitude toward it. If you could choose certain healthy attitudes to rule your life, the ones listed below will make the most difference.

Humility (The Submission Factor)

The attitude of humility is the mind-set that paves the way for all other godly attitudes. Humility means seeing yourself as God sees you—not higher than you are, but not lower either. No matter how important you may look in other people's eyes, you are still microscopic compared with God. The apostle Paul writes:

Have this attitude in yourselves which was also in Christ Jesus, who, although He existed in the form of God, did not regard equality with God a thing to be grasped, but emptied Himself, taking the form of a bond-servant, and being made in the likeness of men. Being found in appearance as a man, He humbled Himself by becoming obedient to the point of death, even death on a cross.

Philippians 2:5–8

A humble attitude produces a heart that wants to serve God and others. A humble person has no problem cheerfully submitting to those in authority. A rebellious person, on the other hand, will get angry with anyone who tells him what to do. Rebellion is always rooted in pride. A humble person cannot be humiliated, but a proud person is constantly offended.

The Bible teaches that everyone is equally valuable in God's eyes, yet we are to regard others as more important. "Do nothing from selfishness or empty conceit, but with humility of mind regard one another as more important than yourselves" (Philippians 2:3).

What are the indications of humility?

SECRET #6

"Change the channel" inside your mind to the Healthy Thoughts Network.

- You are totally dependent upon God and not yourself.
- It does not bother you when you are not recognized for your achievements.
- You are not offended when someone makes a rude remark about you.
- You joyfully serve in lowly jobs because you see yourself working for God.
- You are glad when a fellow worker gets promoted, even if you deserved it more.

- You cheerfully submit to those in authority, even when you do not agree with them.
- You view everyone as important and valuable, and never look down on anyone.
- You refuse to brag about your strengths and accomplishments.
- If someone compliments you for your achievements, you kindly thank them, but you do not let it inflate your ego.

Optimism (The Faith Factor)

Paul said, "I can do all things through Christ who strengthens me" (Philippians 4:13, NKJV). He did not say, "I cannot do anything," nor did he say, "I can do all things through *me* who strengthens me."

Having a positive outlook on life has everything to do with your joy and success. A positive attitude is one that:

- Trusts in the ability of God to come through.
- Refuses to dwell on negative thoughts.
- Sees the best in every situation.
- Speaks uplifting words about others.
- Expects good things to happen.

When Israel was wandering in the wilderness after leaving Egypt, Moses sent twelve men into the land of Canaan to spy on the land, the people and the cities. He wanted to get a sneak preview of where they were going and what they were getting into.

All twelve men looked at the same territory but brought back different reports. Ten spies concluded, "We should not go into the land because we are not able to defeat the giants who live there." Two spies, Joshua and Caleb, said, "We should by all means go up and take possession of it, for we will surely overcome it" (Numbers 13:30). Ten men looked at the Promised Land through pessimist glasses, while two looked at the same territory through optimist glasses.

Everyone is viewing life through one of those pairs of glasses. An optimist searches to find something good in every situation, while a pessimist looks for the worst.

The optimist finds reasons to be happy.
The pessimist finds reasons to be unhappy.
The optimist says, "My cup runs over. What a blessing!"
The pessimist says, "My cup runs over. What a mess!"

People tend to find what they are looking for. If you are looking for faults, you will find them. Miners must move tons of dirt to find an ounce of gold. They are not looking for dirt; they are searching for gold. To find the best in your situation, you must look past the filth and hunt for treasure.

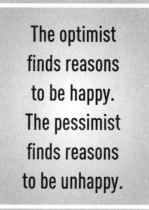

The optimist finds reasons to be happy. The pessimist finds reasons to be unhappy.

I once made a list of 140 positive things to look for in people and circumstances. I printed them on paper and handed them out, saying, "It is too easy to see what is wrong in others. I want you to look for these things in the people you love, but also in your enemies." Before you can see something good, you must first choose to look for and focus on it.

God wants you to have a positive outlook on life and that comes by concentrating on the blessings God has given you.

Scripture instructs us to dwell on uplifting and encouraging thoughts:

> And now, dear brothers and sisters, one final thing. Fix your thoughts on what is true, and honorable, and right, and pure, and lovely, and admirable. Think about things that are excellent and worthy of praise.
>
> Philippians 4:8, NLT

Contentment (The Happiness Factor)

Contentment is the ability to enjoy life regardless of the circumstances. It is choosing to be happy in every situation, embracing your current circumstances and blooming where you are planted.

Contentment is not having everything you want, but wanting everything you have. If you are not happy with what you have, you will not be happy with what you get. The craving that discontentment creates can never be satisfied. It is like a thirsty person who continues to accumulate empty glasses instead of filling the glass he already has. Empty glasses will not quench anyone's thirst. Paul wrote the following statement from a Roman prison:

> I am not saying this because I am in need, for I have learned to be content whatever the circumstances. I know what it is to be in need, and I know what it is to have plenty. I have learned the secret of being content in any and every situation, whether well fed or hungry, whether living in plenty or in want.
>
> Philippians 4:11–12, NIV

Paul said he had to *learn* how to be content. It does not come to us automatically when we turn a certain age. We do not get it through buying another gadget that we think will make us happy. As soon as we get one thing, we will want something else.

It is like the beggar on the street corner who told his friends, "If I only had a hundred dollars, I would never complain again."

A businessman walking by overheard him and said, "Did you say if you had a hundred dollars you would never complain again?"

"You heard right, mister," the beggar replied.

The man handed him a hundred dollars and said, "I'm glad I can bring a little bit of happiness to the world."

After the man walked away, the beggar turned to his friends and said, "Now I wish I had asked for two hundred dollars!"

Did it ever occur to you that the things you now have were once things that you were desperately trying to get? Yet, after you acquired the item, the luster quickly wore off and you started pursuing something else. The attitude of contentment has to be learned.

Contentment is not having everything you want, but wanting everything you have.

Paul also said contentment is a *secret*. Not many people know secrets. If everyone knew, it would not be a secret. When you stop placing conditions on your happiness, you have learned the secret of being content.

Some people live in Never Never Land. They are never happy and never satisfied. Discontentment sends you on an endless search as you run all over the world looking for greener grass. The grass always looks greener on the other side of the fence because you are looking at it from a distance. Once you get over there, you will discover the weeds. You will also find that it needs watering, mowing and fertilizing. Erma Bombeck said, "The grass is always greener over the septic tank."

If you are not content with your situation and you move somewhere else, you are taking the same situation with you to a new location. You will never find happiness in that way. But if you will let the Lord lead you as a shepherd leads sheep, He will make you lie down in *green* pastures (see Psalm 23:2). To "lie down" means to have a restful, contented spirit.

> When you stop placing conditions on your happiness, you have learned the secret of being content.

If you want to be content, you have to quit exposing yourself to all the things the world offers you. Advertising is designed to make you want something that you do not need. I do not need a $100,000 advertisement to entice me to buy something.

Contentment means that you stop envying what other people have. Too many people are miserable because they compare salaries with others and get upset with those making more. God says to be content with your wages (see Luke 3:14). That does not mean that you cannot have a raise or promotion, but it does mean that you will happily live on what you make.

Thankfulness (The Appreciation Factor)

Thankfulness is the attitude that genuinely appreciates God's blessings and expresses gratitude to Him. God deserves far more thanks than He has ever received.

Again Paul writes, "In everything give thanks; for this is God's will for you in Christ Jesus" (1 Thessalonians 5:18). God wants us to be thankful in every circumstance. He does not say, "Be thankful when things are going well for you." He wants us to be thankful every day, all day long. "Always giving thanks for all things in the name of our Lord Jesus Christ to God" (Ephesians 5:20). That is a lifestyle of continually giving thanks throughout each and every day.

Sadly, God hears more complaints than the giving of thanks. Even Christians complain because they think they are entitled to everything from God. Moses warned about developing an ungrateful attitude:

> "When you have eaten and are satisfied, you shall bless the LORD your God for the good land which He has given you. Beware that you do not forget the LORD your God . . . otherwise, when you have eaten and are satisfied [dining in restaurants], and have built good houses and lived in them [a nice home in the suburbs], and when your herds and your flocks multiply [your investments], and your silver and gold multiply [your bank accounts], and all that you have multiplies [even more stuff!], then your heart will become proud and you will forget the LORD your God [complaining]."
>
> Deuteronomy 8:10–14

To "forget the LORD your God" means you stop being thankful. Do you see what God was saying—even to the people back then who had so little? Once all those blessings surround us, it is easy to take them for granted and then we forget to thank God.

When you see the same blessings every day, you eventually stop noticing them.

When you stop noticing them, you stop appreciating them.

When you stop appreciating them, you stop being thankful for them.

When you stop being thankful for them, you start complaining.

At this point, you have forgotten the Lord your God.

127

To develop a thankful attitude, you must increase the value you have placed on your blessings. Everything you own has a price tag in your mind. The value of everything can change according to how much you appreciate it. If you greatly appreciate something, it goes up in value. If it does not mean much to you, it depreciates and goes down in value.

The reason we forget God and become ungrateful is because we have stopped appreciating what we have. This lack of appreciation makes the item, or person, lose value in our eyes. You can have every blessing in the world, but if you do not appreciate them, you will not enjoy them.

It is not what you have, but your attitude toward it that determines its value. How much is a glass of water worth? If you are in a swimming pool, not much. But if you are in a desert, it is worth a fortune. The value of something is not determined by how much it appreciates, but by how much it is appreciated.

Once we start appreciating all the blessings that God has given us, our attitude changes. We stop complaining. We become thankful, which produces joy.

Turning Your Attitude Around

To turn your attitude around, you must begin by deprogramming your mind. First Thessalonians 5:21 says, "But examine everything carefully; hold fast to that which is good."

Paul tells us to examine all our ideas and attitudes, to get rid of the wrong ones and to keep the good ones. But before you can reprogram your mind, you must first deprogram yourself from the toxic thoughts you have been thinking.

Your mind is like a computer and your attitude is the software program that runs your life. If you program your mind with the wrong attitude, it is like a computer virus that causes your computer to malfunction.

I once got a virus on my computer, and it started sending out emails to my friends without my knowledge. Whoever clicked on my email got the virus on their computer, which started emailing their contacts as well. Likewise, a pessimistic, critical attitude will not just affect me, but other people as well.

To get rid of the virus, you need the antivirus program called "repentance" to clean it up. Repentance is the process of deprogramming your mind from wrong thinking. The Greek word for repentance means "to change your mind." In other words, decide in your heart to think differently.

Ask God's forgiveness for your bad attitude. Stop thinking negative, toxic thoughts. When a worrisome thought tries to enter your mind, shut the door and do not let it in. Deprogramming means to shut down the previously ungodly attitudes so they no longer control you.

Reprogramming is installing a new program to run your life, which means changing the way you think. You will never be happy with toxic attitudes, but you can be happy anywhere if you will *decide* to be happy.

You must feed your mind new information. Here are some ways to reprogram your mind so that you will have new attitudes:

- Meditate on God's Word and let it sink in.
- Set your mind on things above where Christ is seated.
- Discipline your mind to keep negative thoughts out.
- Make up your mind to purposely think positive thoughts.
- Yield to the promptings of the Holy Spirit.
- Speak positively about other people.
- Instead of saying, "I am worried," you declare, "I am trusting God with my situation."

If you truly want to change your attitude, you must do it right now. Do not put it off. If you do not make a change today, it is highly unlikely you will do it tomorrow. Your destiny can change, starting at this moment. Will you seize the opportunity?

Discussion Questions

Reprogramming Your Computer

How does a pessimistic attitude affect the way you view others?

What are the two reasons people get angry? What can you do to resolve your anger?

Is it possible to worry and trust God at the same time? Why does one cancel out the other?

Read the list of the indicators of humility and ask yourself if any apply. How can you change your attitude in those areas?

When the twelve men spied out the land of Canaan, why did they bring back two opposite reports? As you "spy out" the land you are now living in, do you see it as a Promised Land or a land ruled by giants?

What is the secret of being content?

What does it mean to "forget the Lord your God"? How can you develop a thankful attitude?

CHALLENGE #7

MANAGING MONEY

Money speaks. It says bye-bye.

—Unknown

Many of the billboards in Florida advertise the lottery and the possibility of winning millions of dollars. Some time ago, I decided to ask God for the numbers to the winning ticket. I figured that if He gave me the number, it would not be gambling but a sure thing. I promised Him that all the money I won would go to missions. When I would get ready for bed, I always put a note pad and pencil on the nightstand, just in case He gave me the numbers in the middle of the night.

One Christmas day, my wife and I planned to fly to North Carolina to be with our family. On the way to the Orlando airport, I noticed a billboard advertising the lottery was now at $60 million for the winning ticket. I prayed and told the Lord that this would be the perfect time to give me the numbers.

Here is what He said to me on that Christmas day: "Son, if I thought money would save the world, I would have sent money instead of My Son. My plan to win the world is to use ordinary people who will express My love and witness to My grace and redemption."

That should have settled it for me, but I still had that lingering feeling that if I just had a lot of money, I could really do a lot of good for Jesus and His Kingdom.

In the United States, "In God We Trust" is written on our coins. If truth be told, it is the money that we really trust. In our society, a person's net worth has become the measure of his security, success and importance. We have bought in to the lie that money can solve all our problems. We believe that if we just had more money, all our troubles would disappear.

Handling money is a challenge for everyone. It is the source of much conflict and the cause of most divorces. Our jails are filled with people who stole or killed to get someone else's money. Some people spend their last few dollars buying lottery tickets, hoping to hit the jackpot. They are looking to everyone but God for provision.

We all naturally look to someone or something to provide our needs. Some people view their employers, government, bank account or stock market as their provider. It is easier to trust something you can see over someone you cannot see.

God wants you to look past the physical realm, and with the eyes of faith, see Him as your provider. His name, Jehovah Jireh, means "the Lord will provide" (see Genesis 22:14). Paul wrote, "And my God will supply all your needs according to His riches in glory in Christ Jesus" (Philippians 4:19). Once we make this shift in our thinking and learn to trust God for everything we need, it sets us free from all worry.

He does not grow money on trees or drop hundred-dollar bills from heaven, but He does use many different avenues to provide for His children. Unfortunately, we sometimes cause our own problems because we mismanage what He has provided. This seventh challenge requires that we learn how to properly handle our money.

Two Purposes for Money

Money in itself is neither good nor bad, but our attitude toward it can be good or bad. "For the love of money is the root of all evil" (1 Timothy 6:10, KJV). Money serves two purposes. It is used as a medium of exchange in this world and it also determines what we will manage in heaven. Planet earth is just a temporary world to prepare us for His everlasting Kingdom.

This life is a test, and only a test. God has assignments in heaven that will last forever, so how will He determine what you will be doing there? God is evaluating your faithfulness in handling your earthly money to decide what you will be assigned in eternity. The way you handle your money is part of that evaluation process. If you are not trustworthy in handling your cash in this life, why would He entrust you with something much more important in the next life?

In biblical times, when a wealthy man was going on a journey, he needed someone to manage his possessions while he was away. The stewards handled the man's buying and selling, just as if he were there doing it himself. When the owner returned from his journey, he evaluated how each steward handled his financial dealings, and then he rewarded them according to their faithfulness. The stewards did not own the money; they simply managed it under the owner's jurisdiction.

Jesus told several parables about stewards, explaining that how we manage the little things in this life will determine what we will oversee in the next life.

"He who is faithful in a very little thing is faithful also in much; and he who is unrighteous in a very little thing is unrighteous also in much. Therefore if you have not been faithful in the use of unrighteous wealth, who will *entrust the true riches* to you?"

Luke 16:10–11, emphasis added

If we are faithful in handling God's money during our lifetimes, He will reward us in the next life with true riches that will last forever. The "true riches" are important responsibilities in heaven, which will be awarded to those who have been good stewards during their earthly lives.

SECRET #7

Handle your money on earth as if it will determine your rewards in heaven.

Since that is the case, it would be wise to take a closer look at the three areas of money management—sowing, spending and saving. Sowing means giving your money in offerings to God and helping others. Spending involves budgeting your expenditures and paying your bills on time. Saving is putting back some cash for emergencies and future expenses. We need to be disciplined in all three areas.

Area #1: Sowing

Jesus said, "It is more blessed to give than to receive" (Acts 20:35). Do you believe that? Proper money management begins with honoring the Lord first with our wealth. Jesus said, "You cannot serve both God and money" (Matthew 6:24, NIV). We must make Him our highest priority in life. He is the "top button." If we get the top button of the shirt right, all the other buttons will fall into place. But if we get the top button in the bottom hole of the shirt, all the rest will be off as well. The same is true with our priorities in money management.

In the city where I live, many financial institutions have printed bumper stickers saying, "I bank smart, do you? I bank at [name of financial institution]." I have made up a bumper sticker that reads, "I bank smart, do you? Lay up treasures in heaven." Jesus gave us this advice, and each one of us needs to seek the Holy Spirit's guidance for the best way to do it.

When you die, you will leave everything behind. I often tell people that the day after they die, their most prized possessions will be sold at a garage sale, given to the Salvation Army or simply dumped in garbage cans. Once you die, your money will mean nothing to you. But you can send treasure up to heaven by giving while you are alive.

> **Giving is easy if we love the object of our gift. But if we do not love the recipient of the gift, giving is extremely difficult.**

Jesus said, "Store up for yourselves treasures in heaven . . . for where your treasure is, *there your heart will be also*" (Matthew 6:20–21, emphasis added). First, He said that it is possible to make deposits in heaven right now. Second, He said that our hearts and our treasure are tied together.

What we do with our money reveals what we love the most. People who love golf have no problem paying for golf clubs, green fees and country club memberships. People who love fishing have no problem buying boats and fishing gear. People who love God have no problem joyfully giving to Him to further His Kingdom.

Giving is easy if we love the object of our gift. But if we do not love the recipient of the gift, giving is extremely difficult. Giving our money to the Lord proves we love Him more than the things we could have bought with it. Our offerings need to be an act of worship from our hearts. If our offerings mean nothing to us, they will mean nothing to God.

When we give to Him, He promises to give back to us.

> Honor the LORD from your wealth and from the *first* of all your produce; so your barns will be filled with plenty and your vats will overflow with new wine.
>
> Proverbs 3:9–10, emphasis added

The Lord wants us to honor Him from the first of what we earn. That means when we get paid, we give our tithes to Him first. A tithe is 10 percent of what you earn and an offering is anything on top of that. He wants us to give our tithes and offerings joyfully to Him, and "not grudgingly or under compulsion, for God loves a cheerful giver" (2 Corinthians 9:7).

If we will honor Him first, He will bless us for doing it: "So that your barns will be filled with plenty and your vats will overflow." The harvest comes at a later time, and God is able to supernaturally increase the yield of your crops and vineyards. That is the God factor, where He gives back to you more than you gave in your offering.

From a human perspective, God's math does not make sense. If you obey what God says, you are going to do a lot of things that do not make sense. When you give 10 percent of your income to God, you actually have less money *at first*. How is it possible for you to live better on 90 percent than you could on 100 percent? It just does not add up. But when the God factor kicks in, you will actually end up with more. And that is not counting your eternal rewards in heaven.

In addition to giving your tithes, the Lord also wants you to give to those in need. The early Church freely gave to each other. "And they began selling their property and possessions and were sharing them with all, as anyone might have need" (Acts 2:45). As we help our brothers and sisters in Christ, it is as if we are giving to the Lord himself. Remember, He is living *inside* the other believer. Jesus said,

> "For I was hungry, and you gave Me *something* to eat; I was thirsty, and you gave Me something to drink. . . . To the extent that you did it to one of these brothers of Mine, even the least of *them*, *you did it to Me*."
>
> Matthew 25:35, 40, emphasis added

When we give to God and others, we need to believe three things.

1. We Must Believe That God Sees What We Give

God is watching us when we give our offerings. When Cain and Abel brought offerings to God, "The LORD had regard for Abel and his offering; but for Cain and for his offering He had no regard" (Genesis 4:4–5). God was not only looking at what they gave, but also at their heart attitude. The Lord told the prophet Malachi that He was displeased with the people's offerings because they were presenting lame and sick animals to Him (see Malachi 1:8). God sees every offering that we give to Him and our attitude while doing it.

2. We Must Believe God Knows about Our Financial Situation

Jesus was once in the Temple watching people put money into the treasury. A poor widow gave her last two coins as an offering to God. Jesus told His disciples:

> "This poor widow put in more than all the contributors to the treasury; for they all put in out of their surplus, but she, out of her poverty, put in all she owned, all she had to live on."
>
> Mark 12:43–44

Jesus knew the financial situation of every contributor. He knew that all gave out of their surplus except the widow. He knew she gave her last two coins and had nothing left. And He knows your financial situation as well.

We do not see Him running to stop her from giving and saying, "Are you crazy? Don't you realize that you're going to starve to death if you give your last two coins?"

Why did He not do that? It was because He knew that her offering released the God factor in her life. God was pleased with her gift and He was not going to let her starve to death.

3. We Must Believe That God Will Reward Our Giving

God promises to open the windows of heaven to pour out a blessing on those who tithe.

> "Bring the whole tithe into the storehouse, so that there may be food in My house, and test Me now in this," says the LORD of hosts, "if I will not open for you the windows of heaven and pour out for you a blessing until it overflows."
>
> Malachi 3:10

Jesus also told us that He would reward our giving.

> "Give, and it will be given to you. They will pour into your lap a good measure—pressed down, shaken together, and running over. For by your standard of measure it will be measured to you in return."
>
> Luke 6:38

While we should not give simply for the purpose of getting back, God does promise to reward our giving. Some rewards will be in this life and some will be in the next life. It takes faith to let go of what we can see to get something we will not see until after we die. After you die, you will see all the treasure that you laid up during your life.

Area #2: Spending

The way we spend our money will determine whether we live in fiscal freedom or in financial bondage. Some people are not satisfied with what they have, so they keep buying more things—and the shopping spree never ends. Hebrews 13:5 tells us, "Make sure that your character is free from the love of money, being content with what you have."

My wife and I believe God called us to a certain standard of living and we are to give the rest of our money away. We give tithes to our local church and offerings as led by the Holy Spirit. We also have a fund in case of emergencies. We have lived in the same house for 43 years and are very happy with it. We do not judge others who have a better lifestyle or a higher standard of living. We have a hard enough time minding our own business.

When people buy more than they can afford, they have violated an important principle of good money management. Overspending is usually rooted in greed. Jesus said, "Beware, and be on your guard against every form of greed; for not even when one has an abundance does his life consist of his possessions" (Luke 12:15).

Here are some tips to help you spend wisely.

Tip 1. Create a Written Budget

A budget is a written plan on how to spend your money. It is your way out of bondage.

Jesus said, "For which of you, intending to build a tower, does not sit down first and count the cost, whether he has enough to finish it" (Luke 14:28, NKJV). Jesus Himself said you need to examine your budget to see whether or not you can afford something. He said if you do not have enough money to build the tower, do not do it.

A budget starts by writing down all your monthly expenses. Get out all your past bills and you can see where your money has gone. Utility companies will usually figure your average monthly payment for you and you can sign up for an "even payment" plan.

> It is not how much you make that determines your debt, but how much you spend.

Write down your average monthly expenses for each category—house or rent payment, utilities, groceries, insurance, car repairs, gasoline, medical and other expenses. You should include tithing and savings in your budget as well.

Add up all your expenses and subtract it from your monthly income. If the net amount is negative, you will either need to cut expenses or figure a way to make more income. If your outgo exceeds your income, your upkeep will be your downfall.

Once you have established your budget, make sure you stick to it. It does no good to make a financial plan if you do not abide by it.

Tip 2. Do Not Buy on Impulse

Impulse buying invariably leads to financial trouble. Proverbs 21:5 says, "Everyone who is hasty comes surely to poverty." Being hasty means to act quickly without thinking about the consequences.

A car salesman said that 95 percent of the cars he sells are bought on impulse. When a customer comes in and gets excited about a particular car, it is as good as sold. Many of these people buy items that they really cannot afford because their emotions are overruling common sense. As a result, they just get deeper in debt.

One way you can stop impulse buying is to leave the store, go home, pray about the decision and sleep on it. This will help you make wise decisions and keep you from buying things you do not need. By the next day, your emotions will have settled down and you might not even remember how badly you wanted it because the desire will be gone.

Tip 3. Live within Your Means

Your yearnings cannot exceed your earnings. Stop spending more than you make. It is not how much you make that determines your debt, but how much you spend. I know of a man who made $120,000 a year but could not make ends meet. He lived in a small rental house but had massive debt on credit cards; he did not have enough saved to live even one month.

You live within your means by cutting your expenses and simplifying your lifestyle. Eat at home rather than going to restaurants all the time. Buy a cheaper plan on your cell phone. Drop cable television if you cannot afford it. Downsize and live in a smaller place. Make repairs on your old car instead of buying a new one. Cut out all unnecessary expenses.

We are all bombarded with advertising that tries to persuade us that we "need" what they have to offer. Learn to distinguish between your wants and needs. You would be surprised by how much you can live without.

My wife and I were both brought up in families that were very frugal, so we learned to live with less at an early age. In addition, my salary as a young minister was barely enough to live on. We did not use credit cards to get by. If we needed something, we paid cash for it. We lived within our means by sacrificing and living very modestly.

With that said, frugality must not always be the rule. The Holy Spirit should guide you in the decisions you make.

Remember the woman who anointed Jesus with a very expensive bottle of perfume. The disciples rebuked her, telling her the money could have been given to the poor. Jesus corrected them and commended her for her sacrificial gift.

My wife and I were invited out to eat by a friend to a restaurant where the steaks cost $150. At first I refused to go because I thought no one should pay that much for a steak. Then the Holy Spirit convicted me that this man was just trying to bless us. If I refused to go, it would keep him from doing something he truly wanted to do for us. We did go out to dinner with him, although I could not bring myself to order the $150 steak. Instead, I ordered a less expensive item.

So live within your means, but do not feel guilty when you go on vacation or to a nice restaurant. God wants you to enjoy life by living on what He provides and being thankful for all things.

Tip 4. Get Out of Debt

Thirty million Americans are behind in their credit card payments, and the average credit card debt per household is $15,788. Because interest compounds over time, it will take about thirty years to pay off $2,000 on your credit card if you only make the minimum payment.

If it takes three decades to pay off $2,000, how long will it take to pay off $15,788? It will take your entire lifetime, unless you decide to do something about it. You will never dig yourself out of the hole if you only pay the minimum amount each month. To get out of debt you must aggressively pay extra on the principal.

The more you owe, the more you are owned. "The rich rules over the poor, and the borrower becomes the lender's slave" (Proverbs 22:7). God does not want us to be in financial bondage, but to pay off our debts. Psalm 37:21 says, "The wicked borrows and does not pay back, but the righteous is gracious and gives." You know you are in debt when your credit card number and the amount you owe are the same number!

If you pay off your entire credit card debt every month, it is fine to use them. If you do not pay off the balance every month, however, you forfeit the right to use them. You must perform "plastic surgery" and cut them up! By destroying your cards, it keeps you from automatically buying things you cannot afford. Start paying for everything in cash and you will think twice about purchasing the item.

The more you owe, the more you are owned.

Financial counselor Larry Burkett became a Christian at our church. At that time, he worked at the space program at Cape Canaveral. He left the program to start Christian Financial Concepts, which became a nationwide ministry. He devoted his life to teaching people how to budget and get out of debt.

When he challenged us to get debt-free, my wife and I accepted his challenge. We had to bite the bullet to do it, but over the past thirty years we have paid less than two hundred dollars in interest. We have never made a six-figure salary, but the Lord has always provided for us, and we have been able to give so much more, even in our retirement.

Some other members of our church took the challenge to get out of debt. One young couple with four young children became completely debt-free. Another couple retired early because they did not owe anything to anyone.

The only way to get out of debt is to stop spending so much and to pay extra on the principal, which cuts down the time it takes to pay off the debt. Because credit cards usually charge the highest interest rates, it is best to pay them off before the lower interest debts.

Getting Out of Debt

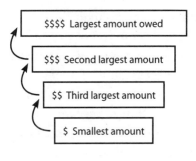

| $$$$ Largest amount owed |
| $$$ Second largest amount |
| $$ Third largest amount |
| $ Smallest amount |

Pay off smallest debt first and then work on the next smallest amount.

Make a list of your debts and start with the smallest one first. When paying that bill each month, add an extra amount marked "extra principal." Once you get rid of that obligation, work on the next smallest debt. Once you pay off that debt, work your way up the list until all debts are paid off.

> The only way to get out of debt is to stop spending so much and by paying extra on the principal.

Use this same strategy of paying extra principal with your home mortgage. When you make your monthly payment, think of the principal part as *your* money and the interest part as the bank's money. As you can see from the chart, although your payment stays the same every month, the principal and interest change. As you make extra principal payments, view it as money that you are saving in your "house account."

The chart is for a $150,000 thirty-year mortgage at 5 percent. When you make payment #1 ($805.23), if you will add an extra $180.98 to it (the principal for the second month), it will make your total payment $986.21, but you will save $624.25 in interest. Your balance now drops to $149,638.78. The next month when you make your $805.23 payment, if you will add $182.49 (the principal payment #4), the total will be $987.72, but you will save another $622.74 in interest. Your balance is now $149,274.55. If you will continue to pay the next month's principal with each payment, you will pay off your house in fifteen years instead of thirty. Do you now see how paying extra on the principal cuts down on the time that it takes to pay it off?

Amortization Schedule
$150,000 thirty-year mortgage at 5%

Months	Payment	Principal	Interest	Balance due
1	$805.23	$180.23	$625.00	$149,819.77
2	$805.23	$180.98	$624.25	$149,638.78
3	$805.23	$181.74	$623.49	$149,457.05
4	$805.23	$182.49	$622.74	$149,274.55
5	$805.23	$183.25	$621.98	$149,091.30
357	$805.23	$791.95	$13.28	$2,395.72
358	$805.23	$795.25	$9.98	$1,600.47
359	$805.23	$798.56	$6.67	$801.91
360	$805.23	$801.89	$3.34	$0.01

It is wiser, however, to pay the most extra principal at the beginning of your loan rather than at the end. Take a look at payment #359, which is the month before you completely pay off your mortgage. Your monthly payment is still $805.23, but you would have to pay an extra $798.56 to knock off one additional month. But if you will pay an extra $798.56 in principal with your *first* payment, it will reduce the time you would pay by about four and a half months! It makes no sense to pay extra on the principal at the end of your loan because most of your payment goes to principal anyway. (See payments #357–#360.)

A friend of mine paid off his thirty-year home mortgage in eleven years by paying extra on principal. For six years he paid extra on the principal every month and reduced the loan from thirty years to five years. He then quit paying extra money for those last five years because virtually all those remaining payments went to principal.

If you sell your house before paying it off, you will get back all the principal that you have paid because it is your equity in the home.

I strongly advise that you get a printout of your amortization schedule, which will show the amount of principal and interest for every payment of your loan. As you make each extra payment, mark the balance on your schedule so that you can *see* how many months you have knocked off. Keeping track of how much time you have reduced your mortgage will help you stay motivated to continue doing it. If you do not keep track of your progress, you will probably lose your motivation and will quit doing it.

Where does the extra money come from to make these additional payments?

- Sell items you do not need.
- Cut out unnecessary expenses such as dining out or hobbies.
- Use your income tax refund to pay off debt.
- If you have expensive car payments, sell it and drive an older vehicle.

• Get rid of cable television and expensive cell phone plans.
• Stop buying junk food.

You *can* get out of debt if you set your mind to do it. "Do not withhold good from those to whom it is due, when it is in your power to do it" (Proverbs 3:27). It will take discipline and sacrifice, but you will be amazed at the burden that is lifted off you.

Area #3: Savings

During the Depression in the 1930s, the average person saved 3 percent of their income. Today the savings rate is negative 1 percent, which means that people are spending more than they earn.

One of the main reasons we need to save is so we can pay for items without having to borrow. "There is precious treasure and oil in the dwelling of the wise, but a foolish man swallows it up" (Proverbs 21:20). If you need to buy furniture or anything else, save up the money and then pay for it instead of putting it on your credit card.

God wants us to save money, but He does not want us to save with the wrong motives. One wrong motive for saving is reliance on money rather than God. "Instruct those who are rich in this present world not to be conceited or to fix their hope on the uncertainty of riches, but on God" (1 Timothy 6:17).

Stinginess can also be a wrong motive. A miser is a person who saves money but does not want to spend or give it away. When we give to God and others, it keeps us from becoming selfish, miserly people.

With those wrong motives aside, God's Word tells us some good reasons to save:

Reason #1: To Establish an Emergency Fund

We need to be prepared for emergencies. The car breaks down. The roof leaks. How would you get by if you lost your job?

Financial counselors suggest that we should have saved enough in the emergency fund to live for three to six months. To save that amount, we will need to sacrifice some things now to create that safety net.

"A prudent person foresees danger and takes precautions. The simpleton goes blindly on and suffers the consequences" (Proverbs 27:12, NLT). A wise person thinks ahead and prepares for possible emergencies. When God leads us to prepare for what might happen, it gives us peace and keeps us from being afraid.

Jesus told a parable about ten virgins waiting for a wedding ceremony, which got delayed. Five of the young women were wise because they brought enough oil, but the other five were foolish because they were unprepared for the unforeseen delay. They missed the wedding procession because they had not thought ahead about what might happen (see Matthew 25:1–10).

God revealed to Pharaoh through Joseph that Egypt would have seven years of abundant crops, which would be followed by seven years of famine. Joseph instructed Pharaoh to save during the abundant years to prepare for the lean years (see Genesis 41:1–36). Can you imagine what would have happened if Pharaoh decided to spend his seven years of profits on extravagant living instead of saving it? Egypt and Israel would have perished.

Ants have brains one-tenth the size of a pinhead, yet they are wiser than some people. "Four things on earth are small, yet they are extremely wise: Ants are creatures of little strength, yet they store up their food in the summer" (Proverbs

30:24–25, NIV). They wisely store up food during the summer because that is when things are growing. Even with their tiny brains, they have enough sense to know that winter is coming when nothing will grow, and so they prepare during the time of abundance for the lean season.

Reason #2: To Leave an Inheritance for Your Children

You have probably seen the bumper sticker that says, "I'm spending my kids' inheritance." Although that phrase brings laughs, God wants us to help the future generations in our family who will be following us. To bequeath an estate means you have accumulated some assets over your lifetime. "A good man leaves an inheritance to his children's children" (Proverbs 13:22).

"Children are not obligated to save up for their parents, but parents for their children" (2 Corinthians 12:14, ESV). Most people need the help of an inheritance to move forward in life. Hopefully your children will be wise money managers so they can pass it along to their children and grandchildren as well.

Reason #3: To Have Money Available to Help Others in Need

God blesses us financially with surplus so we can help others who have less.

Right now you have plenty and can help those who are in need. Later, they will have plenty and can share with you when you need it. In this way, things will be equal.

2 Corinthians 8:14, NLT

This is God's way of making things even.

Giving to those in the family of God is a high priority. "Let us do good to all people, and especially to those who are of the household of the faith" (Galatians 6:10). Be generous to those in need, but also be discerning.

If you suspect that a supposedly needy person on the street is a con artist who is trying to extract money from you, you do not have to help him. Jesus said, "Do not give what is holy to the dogs; nor cast your pearls before swine, lest they trample them under their feet, and turn and tear you in pieces" (Matthew 7:6, NKJV). Just because a person claims to be in need does not mean that it is true. Scripture repeatedly warns us, "Do not be deceived" (James 1:16). If you feel uneasy about helping someone off the street, give that amount instead to a charitable organization that you do trust to help the needy.

Finding Money to Save

Where do you find the money to save? Again, you can cut your expenses. Whenever you want to buy something, ask yourself, *Do I really need this?* You would be surprised how many things you do not really need. Clark Howard's book, *Living Large in Lean Times*, lists over 250 ways to save money and live within your means.

You can cut expenses by turning off lights when no one is in the room. Sell items that you do not need. Wait to buy items when they go on sale.

Stick to your shopping list at the grocery store and do not pick up things that are not on it. Use grocery coupons. You can get coupons online and in the newspaper.

Buy used instead of new. You can get pre-owned items from books to furniture online for a fraction of the cost. When you shop at garage sales, go to the nicest neighborhoods because they are trying to get rid of quality items and often do not put high prices on them.

Now you have enough information to handle your money wisely. But you will never be able to do it until you decide in your heart to make it happen.

Discussion Questions

Dividing Your Dollars

Why is it important to honor the Lord *first* when you get paid? (See Proverbs 3:9–10.)

What did Jesus mean when He said, "Therefore if you have not been faithful in the use of unrighteous wealth, who will entrust true riches to you?" (Luke 16:11).

Discuss the statement, "Giving is easy if we love the object of our gift. But if we do not love the recipient of the gift, giving is extremely difficult." Do you think this is true? Why or why not?

What do you think God saw in Cain and Abel, and how did that affect His receptiveness to their offerings? (See Genesis 4:4–5.)

What does it mean to "live within your means"? Are you doing it?

What are the two things necessary to get out of debt?

Discuss why it is important to have an emergency fund.

TRUSTING THROUGH TRIALS

Life is full of obstacle illusions.

—Grant Frazier

I know a man who was falsely accused by his wife of molesting their daughter. All it takes to destroy someone's reputation is to put a question mark in people's minds that the false allegations *might* be true. Even though he was innocent, he was treated shamefully by the court system and locked up in jail.

How would you feel if you were placed in that situation? Being falsely maligned of such a despicable act would have to be one of the most stressful trials anyone could face. This man continued to trust God that the truth would come to light. Miraculously, indisputable evidence came forth proving that the accusations were contrived and he was innocent. He was cleared of the charges and released from jail.

He has faithfully attended Bible study and discipleship groups, which has kept him from becoming bitter over having his reputation smeared. I have often wondered if I would have done as well as he has if that had happened to me.

Trials can be nerve-racking, especially if we do not handle them correctly. So often we want to run from the problem, or sweep it under the rug, pretending it will go away. If the trial is life threatening, it sends us into panic mode, just like the disciples became unglued when they encountered a storm.

Jesus was crossing over the Sea of Galilee with His disciples and sleeping in the back of the boat when a fierce storm hit. Huge waves were crashing over the side. The boat was quickly filling up with water as Jesus slept soundly on a cushion, seemingly unaware that the vessel was in danger of sinking (see Mark 4:35–41).

We panic when we can no longer control our circumstances.

Jesus never warned His disciples about a storm coming, so they were not expecting one. Their calm evening cruise turned into "fright night" on the sea. Their boat was on the verge of sinking, and the terrified disciples realized this problem was too big for them to handle.

Like all storms, trials come to us in varying degrees of intensity. Big storms make big waves. Little storms make little waves. Some trials create ripples, while other storms produce tidal waves. The tsunamis are storms that terrify us.

Picture the situation. Waves are crashing over the side of the boat as the disciples are frantically trying to bail water out. Another huge wave breaks over the rim and more water rushes in. It will not be long until the ship and crew go under.

If anyone on the planet could help them get out of their jam, it was Jesus. With their own eyes the disciples had seen Jesus cast out demons, heal lepers and make a paralyzed man walk. At an earlier time, Jesus ordered so many fish to swim into their nets that the nets started breaking—and it happened on the same sea that was now threatening to swallow them up. And the God of the universe, who did all those miracles, just happens to be riding in the backseat.

The troubled twelve rush to the stern and they cannot believe their eyes. Jesus' head is propped up on a pillow and water is up to His neck, but He is asleep! Since this was the lowest place in the boat, it was the first to fill up with water. How can He be snoozing when waves are crashing on Him? The disciples stare at each other in disbelief when they realize the captain of their ship is asleep at the wheel.

If you were a passenger in a car where the driver was asleep at the wheel, you would be frightened too. We panic when we can no longer control our circumstances.

It was no accident that He was sleeping during that storm. This is the only incident in the Bible where it specifically states that Jesus was asleep. But why is He napping during the storm? What does God want us to see?

We know that Jesus did not do anything except for what His Father told Him to do (see John 5:19). He fell asleep because He was obeying what the Father said.

He is snoring in the stern—even though He is sopping wet. The boat is acting like a roller coaster, and the shipmates are screaming in fear, but Jesus is at perfect peace. The disciples shook Him out of His slumber, yelling, "Do You not care that we are going to drown?"

If you could choose a situation where it looked like God was not in control, this was it. But this was a laboratory experiment to teach His disciples—and us—that He is still in control, even when our world is falling apart.

Whenever we go through a storm, our faith gets tested to see what we really believe. Are we going to be at peace and go to sleep, knowing that God is in control in the midst of our difficulty? Or, are we going to panic because the problem seems much too big for Him to handle?

We Are All in the Same Boat

This wild ride on the Sea of Galilee is an object lesson for our trials as well, and we are all in the same boat. Like the storm that hit the disciples' boat, our trials often hit us without warning. Just as the waves crashed in on them, our problems crash in on us. In the same way the disciples panicked while Jesus slept, we panic when it appears God is unaware of our predicament.

Our storms may not consist of wind and waves, but they may look like this:

Financial storms. We do not have enough money to pay our monthly bills.

Health storms. The doctor gives us a bad prognosis without much hope.

Family storms. Our child rebels or our spouse decides to leave.

Relationship storms. Trying to get along with unkind people who will not reciprocate.

Employment storms. Searching for a job but no doors are opening.

Bereavement storms. Losing a loved one through death.

When your boat is filling up with water, what are you to do? Grab more buckets? Put on your life preserver? Scream at the sleeping Messiah?

So often when we go through a trial, we want to know *why* it is happening to us. One man was going through every kind of trial imaginable. He shook his fist at the sky and screamed, "Why me, God? Why?"

Immediately the clouds split apart and a voice thundered from heaven, "Because some people just tick me off!"

It is unlikely that the trial you are going through is because God is ticked off. But let's be honest—knowing why you are going through a difficulty really does not make it any easier. God is not going to write a message in the sky, explaining why horrible things are happening to you. Instead, He simply asks you to trust Him.

Deuteronomy 29:29 says, "The secret things belong to the LORD our God, but the things revealed belong to us and to our sons forever." Our unanswered questions are those secret things that belong to the Lord. He is not going to tell us those secret things in this life, but when we stand before Him in the next life, He promises to answer our every question. The apostle Paul said, "Now I know in part, but then *I will know fully* just as I also have been fully known" (1 Corinthians 13:12, emphasis added). God promises to explain in detail how and why everything happened on earth the way it did.

Until that day arrives, you must continue to trust Him, even when you do not understand. King Solomon gave this wise bit of advice: "Trust in the LORD with all your heart and do not lean on your own understanding" (Proverbs 3:5). Stop trying to figure out why your trial is happening and who is responsible. You can drive yourself crazy if you do that.

Trials can come from various sources, so it is wrong to blame everything that happens on either God or the devil. Many people cause their own problems due to the bad choices they have made.

Headstrong people can also cause you problems. Satan can influence people to do evil by planting suggestions in their minds, with you as the intended target. Some trials are the result of the natural laws operating in the world. If you fall from a tree, God is not going to suspend the law of gravity to protect you, although He may soften the landing.

God often gets blamed for things He did not do. Disastrous acts of nature such as tornadoes are often given the misnomer "acts of God" rather than "acts of the devil." Satan tries to contaminate our faith by getting us to blame God.

In the book of Job, Satan caused the tragedies in Job's life, but the devil wanted him to blame it on God (see Job 1:9–22; 2:1–9). After Satan destroyed Job's property and health, Mrs. Job tried to get her husband to accuse God. "Curse God and die," she suggested (Job 2:9). She never realized that Satan was the real culprit behind the tragedies and she was his mouthpiece.

Car accidents occur because a driver was not paying attention or the road was slippery, and not because God caused it to happen. I read about a woman who gave her teenage son a car. The youth enjoyed driving recklessly and racing around curves. One day as he was speeding, his car skidded off the road and he crashed into a telephone pole. He was thrown through the windshield and was rushed to a hospital. When their pastor arrived at the hospital, the mother rushed up to him and exclaimed, "Why would God let this happen?"

We often blame the Lord for "letting" something happen when we are the ones at fault. We make wrong assumptions about God—that He either caused it to happen or should have prevented it, which makes us direct our anger at Him.

When a tragedy occurs, the devil tries to poison our faith by suggesting God caused it to happen; therefore, He must not be good. We do not stop believing in God, but we begin to question whether or not He is a good God. Yet, the Scriptures repeatedly affirm God's goodness: "The LORD is good to all" (Psalm 145:9). John tells us, "God is love" (1 John 4:8). Jesus said He is even "kind to ungrateful and evil men" (Luke 6:35).

During times of calamity, we must not let the pain of the moment distort our concept of God's loving and kind nature.

The storms of life do not come because God is taking shots at us from heaven. They are usually the result of someone's poor choices, the violation of God-ordained principles, or simply because trials are a part of life. Jesus said, "In the world you will have tribulation" (John 16:33, NKJV). As long as we live on this planet, we will all experience difficulties.

The Testing of Your Faith

Jesus' brother James wrote, "Consider it all joy, my brethren, when you encounter various trials, knowing that the testing of your faith produces endurance" (James 1:2–3). This verse tells us that every trial is also a test of our faith, which will reveal whether or not we are going to trust God.

Faith is simply a theory until it passes a test, and that test will show us what is inside our hearts.

> "You shall remember all the way which the LORD your God has led you in the wilderness these forty years, that He might humble you, *testing you, to know what was in your heart,* whether you would keep His commandments or not."
>
> Deuteronomy 8:2, emphasis added

Although God knows what is in our hearts, we really do not understand what is inside us until something forces it out. God will allow people or circumstances to shake us to reveal what is inside.

A man building a fence hit his thumb with a hammer and started cursing. He told his friend, "I'm sorry. That really wasn't in me."

His friend replied, "It had to be in you, or it wouldn't have come out of you."

If you shake a cup of liquid, what comes out? Whatever is inside. If orange juice is in the glass, orange juice comes out. If vinegar is inside, vinegar comes out.

Trials will shake us so that whatever is inside our hearts comes spilling out. God lets our hidden feelings come to the surface so that we can see them for ourselves and correct our wrong attitudes.

When You Are Going through a Storm

Perhaps you are in the middle of a storm and your boat is filling up with water. What should you do?

Keep a positive attitude, trusting that God will work it out for your good. Here are four things you must do to get through your crisis.

1. Submit Yourself to His Lordship

SECRET #8

Ask God to control your life and then He will control your circumstances.

Before you can trust God to take care of your storm, you must ask Him to be your Lord. Do not ask God to control the events in your life until you first ask Him to control your life.

God will give you the grace to get through your trial. Some difficulties will require greater grace than others. The greater the hardship, the greater the grace required. James writes, "But He gives *a greater grace.* Therefore *it* says, 'God is opposed to the proud, but gives grace to the humble.' Submit therefore to God" (James 4:6–7, emphasis added).

Notice that God will oppose those who arrogantly believe they do not need Him. Do you want the Lord to be against you? If not, submit to His lordship.

2. Remind God of His Promises

God gave promises in His Word to keep us from panicking. Jesus said, "Do not let your heart be troubled, nor let it be fearful" (John 14:27). Whenever we let our heart be troubled and afraid, we panic. Instead, we must rest on the promises He gave us.

Before they set sail, Jesus told His disciples, "Let us go *over* to the other side" (Mark 4:35, emphasis added). He did not say, "Let us go under." Nor did He say, "Let us go halfway over and then we will sink to the bottom."

Although the disciples did not realize it at the time, Jesus pledged to them before they got into the boat that they would arrive safely on the other side. If they would have remembered His promise when the waves were crashing in, it would have given them assurance that everything would turn out all right.

A friend of mine told me that he ordered a pizza and handed the female cashier a coupon for $3 off. She said, "I'm sorry but we can't take this."

"The coupon says Pizza Hut," he replied. "This is Pizza Hut, isn't it?"

She answered, "Yes, this is Pizza Hut, but the coupon has expired."

The coupon was void due to the expiration date, but God's promises are always good. Even though His promises were written several thousand years ago, they are still in effect today. "For no matter how many promises God has made, they are 'Yes' in Christ. And so through him the 'Amen' is spoken by us to the glory of God" (2 Corinthians 1:20, NIV).

God wants us to present our "coupons" to Him by reminding Him of His promises. Moses, David and others reminded God of what He had said. When you are going through a trial, you can say:

"Lord, You said in Matthew 6:34 to not worry about to-morrow, so I am going to trust You to take care of it."

"Lord, You told me in Hebrews 13:5 that You will never fail me or forsake me."

"Lord, You said in Philippians 4:19 You would provide all my needs."

"Lord, You said in Jeremiah 1:12 that You are watching over Your Word to perform it."

"Lord, You promised in Psalm 84:11 that no good thing would You withhold from those who walk uprightly."

The fulfilling of the promise does not depend on you, but on the God who made the promise. Trust is taking a person at his word. God says, "If you are going through a trial and do not know what to do, ask Me and I will give you wisdom and show you" (see James 1:5). The Lord will show you how to advance through whatever challenges you face.

3. Put Your Complete Trust in the Lord

One of the biggest storms I have been through was when one of our sons got involved in drugs. It hurt us deeply when he got arrested and put in jail. It seemed as though our prayers were not being heard, but God was doing things in our son's heart that we could not see. Sometimes the people we pray for must first hit bottom before they will look up.

My wife and I continued to trust God to intervene, even though the storm looked more threatening than when we first started praying. The Lord Jesus Christ was using this situation to get my attention so I would desperately seek Him in a much deeper way.

God used the trouble to get our son to look upward, and he repented of his rebellion. He became a Christian, later attended theological seminary, and is now the senior pastor of the church where I was pastor for thirty years. One of the valuable lessons I learned through this was that I must trust Him with all my heart and I cannot be swayed by how menacing the storm may look at the moment.

If the storm in your life is getting out of control, instead of panicking, shift your dependence to God. You cannot panic and trust God at the same time. To put your trust in God, you must stop trusting in yourself. A person who trusts in himself is like a man who represents himself in a court of law. He has a fool for a client and a fool for a lawyer. Trust means to let God be your attorney and represent you.

The reason you cannot understand why you are going through your trial is because you are trying to make an evaluation when you do not know all the facts. There is more to what you are going through than what meets the eye, and God is not going to explain it because it would not make sense anyway. This forces you to trust Him, even when you do not understand. When you put your complete trust in God, you will stop trying to figure everything out.

> When you put your complete trust in God, you will stop trying to figure everything out.

King David went through more trials and difficulties than you will probably ever experience. Here is what he did in trying circumstances: "When I am afraid, I will put my trust in You. . . . In God I have put my trust; I shall not be afraid" (Psalm 56:3–4). He *put* his trust in God.

To "put" means to transfer from one place to another. When you put gasoline into your car, you transfer it from the pump to the gas tank. When you put valuables in your safety deposit box, you transfer them from your home to the bank. Therefore, when you put your trust in the Lord, you transfer your faith from yourself to Him.

Trust means you place your burden on God rather than carrying it yourself. Trust is having *confidence in another person.* You can only trust God as much as you know Him and His promises. It is impossible to trust God if you do not believe that He is good and has your best interest at heart.

> It is impossible to trust God if you do not believe that He is good and has your best interest at heart.

David also said, "O taste and see that the LORD is good" (Psalm 34:8). Tasting has to be done by each person individually. The only way you will know what something tastes like is if you try it for yourself. If you believe that God is good and that He wants the best for you, you will have peace because you are letting Him take care of your problem.

4. Believe That God Is in Control, Even When Things Look Out of Control

God's Word says, "The LORD has established His throne in the heavens, and His sovereignty rules over all" (Psalm 103:19). God rules the world, but that does not mean He causes everything to happen. He does not cause people to sin and do perverted things. God's sovereignty means that He gives everyone a free will, but He sets limits on what can and cannot happen. It also means He works all things together for good to those who love Him (see Romans 8:28).

When the storm hit, the disciples became terrified because they did not believe that God was in control of the storm.

Jesus was asleep, and if they had not awoken Him, He would have slept through the entire storm.

I cannot imagine Jesus waking up, rubbing His eyes, and saying, "Whoa! I had no idea that this storm was about to sink the boat. Why didn't you guys wake Me up sooner?"

Jesus could go to sleep because He knew that His Father was in control, even when He was not awake. To settle His disciples down, Jesus commanded the wind and the waves to become calm, and immediately the storm stopped.

> He got up and rebuked the wind and said to the sea, "Hush, be still." And the wind died down and it became perfectly calm. And He said to them, "Why are you afraid? Do you still have no faith?"
>
> Mark 4:39–40

This supernatural act proved that He was in control and had authority over the storm.

But was God in control of the storm *before* Jesus made it stop? Was He in control while He was sleeping and waves were crashing over the sides? The answer is yes. Jesus had complete trust that His Father was controlling the size of the waves and the amount of water in the boat.

In eternity past, God planned that His Son would die on the cross. Peter said, "This Man, delivered over by *the predetermined plan and foreknowledge of God*, you nailed to a cross by the hands of godless men and put Him to death" (Acts 2:23, emphasis added).

Since Jesus knew this was how He was going to die, He was not worried about the boat sinking. God's plan was for Him to be crucified on the cross, not to drown in the sea. The crucifixion was determined before Christ was born, which was prophesied in the Scriptures. God controlled the world's events so that all the prophecies about Him would come to pass. If God can control historical events so that prophecies are fulfilled, it also' means He was in control of that storm on the Sea of Galilee.

How are you going to ride out your next storm? Will you panic and be terrified, or will you completely trust God to get you to the other side?

Discussion Questions

Weathering Your Storms

Discuss a crisis that you have been through that caused you to panic.

Why do you think the Father told Jesus to sleep during that storm? How does that apply to the crises we go through?

Read Deuteronomy 8:2. How do trials reveal what is inside our hearts?

Why is it essential to submit ourselves completely to God during a storm?

Jesus said, "Do not let your heart be troubled, nor let it be fearful" (John 14:27). How do we "let" our hearts become troubled and afraid?

How can reminding God of His promises help us to get through a trial?

What does it mean to "put" your trust in God?

Read Psalm 103:19. Why is it important to believe in God's sovereignty when circumstances appear to be out of control?

SUBMITTING TO AUTHORITIES

Many refuse to accept the reality of a personal God because they are unwilling to submit to His authority.

—Kurt Bruner

Your boss is impossible to work for and makes unreasonable demands from his employees. You are angry at the government's wasteful spending and are tempted to cheat on your taxes. You do not agree with some of the decisions your church leaders have made. What should you do?

God softly whispers, *Submit*. Only those with sensitive hearts will hear it.

Submission is one of the most despised words in today's world. Partly because we misunderstand its meaning, but mainly because we do not want to do it.

We live in a society that loves to ridicule its leaders. Late night show comedians beat up on the president. Kids bad-mouth their teachers. Teenagers detest their parents. Employees belittle their bosses. No respect for authority.

But submission is not a curse word. In God's dictionary, submission is the key that opens the door to God's blessing, and it is the ninth challenge you will face.

The Greek word for *submit* means "to yield under authority." It is a Greek military term meaning "to arrange troop divisions in a military fashion under the command of a leader." It is an attitude of the heart that voluntarily gives respect to those in higher positions.

Submission yields the right-of-way to authorities. When you and another driver arrive at a four-way stop at the same time, the law dictates that you yield the right-of-way to the car on your right. Submission is yielding the right-of-way to a person in authority over you.

> **Submission is yielding the right-of-way to a person in authority over you.**

Every Christian must understand authority since it is the basis for our relationship with the Lord Jesus Christ. When we accept Jesus as Lord, we surrender to Him the right to direct our lives. Anyone who does not have an intimate relationship with Christ will have a hard time submitting.

Everyone either *respects* authority or *resents* authority. The choice you make will say a great deal about your relationship with the Lord. Selfishness always wants to put itself first and demands its own way. A rebellious person is an individual who resists authority instead of submitting to it.

God hates rebellion against authority, which is nothing more than witchcraft and idolatry. "For rebellion is as the sin of witchcraft, and stubbornness is as iniquity and idolatry" (1 Samuel 15:23, NKJV).

Most of us would not dabble in witchcraft. We would not think of worshipping idols. But this verse says that rebellion is the same as witchcraft and idolatry. Witchcraft is an unholy spirit that wants to be in control. Idolatry is worship of a false deity. God clearly detests rebellion and will not bless those who fight against authorities.

Some people move from job to job and church to church—always angry with the people in charge. They want those authorities to submit to their wishes rather than vice versa. They may even hold the correct opinion about the issues so dear to them, but they never realize their attitude toward authority is more important to God than pushing their own agendas.

The Principles of Submission

Principles are facts about the way things work that explain causes and effects. It is vital that we understand from God's viewpoint how authority and submission operate, and the causes and effects related to each.

Until we understand and follow the principles of submission, we will never grow spiritually. We will never have the power that we need in our lives. We will never receive God's full blessing or function effectively in ministry. Our house will never be in order.

Here are six principles of submission that every Christian must grasp.

Principle #1: God Has Established Human Institutions to Be in Authority over Us and He Wants Us to Submit to Them

God set up governments and authorities to put order in our lives. Can you imagine the chaos if no one was in charge and no one was accountable to anyone else? The Lord could have made us all independent spirits, where everyone was their own authority, but the world would be in more trouble than it is now. To keep this from happening, He established governments and human institutions to rule on earth.

Submit yourselves for the Lord's sake to every human institution, whether to a king as the one in authority, or to governors as sent by him for the punishment of evildoers and the praise of those who do right.

1 Peter 2:13–14

It is easy to convince ourselves that we are submitting to the Lord, while at the same time rebelling against the human institutions that He has established. When we submit to earthly authorities, we are submitting to God. Four truths are explained in this verse:

How to Submit

"Submit yourselves." The only one who can submit "yourself" is *yourself*. No one else can do it for you. It is a decision that you must make.

Motive for Submitting

"For the Lord's sake." You submit to human institutions because you love and respect the Lord. You are doing it to honor the higher authority, God, who has established the human authorities. You look past human flesh to see divinity, and submit in spite of the imperfections of the earthly institutions.

To Whom to Submit

"Every human institution." This includes government, jobs, churches and families. Submission touches every area of our lives. We are to submit to kings, who are the highest authority in a nation, and to governors, who are the representatives of the king.

WHY WE NEED TO SUBMIT

Authorities are trying to keep order in the world. They punish those who do wrong and honor those who do right. When Paul and Peter wrote their letters, Rome was ruling the world. Although the Roman government was corrupt in many ways, Christians were instructed to submit to it.

God chooses to work through the authorities He has established on earth. The book of James says, "Is anyone among you sick? Let him call for the elders of the church, and let them pray over him, anointing him with oil in the name of the Lord" (James 5:14, NKJV).

But why call the elders? Cannot anyone pray for someone else?

Of course they can. This verse, however, indicates that healing comes through submission to His established authorities in the church. God sends His healing power down from heaven, using the church leaders as His conduit. When a sick person calls on the elders for prayer, that individual recognizes their authority and submits to them, which releases healing into them.

Principle #2: Submit to Authorities, Even When They Are Unfair

In the Old Testament, Abraham's wife, Sarai, treated her maid Hagar harshly, which caused her employee to flee (see Genesis 16:6–10). That is the natural reaction, isn't it? When someone in authority treats you harshly, it is tempting to quit.

The angel of the Lord found Hagar in the wilderness and told her, "Return to your mistress, and *submit yourself to her authority*" (Genesis 16:9, emphasis added).

I am sure that Hagar said, "I know you saw me hiding in this wilderness, but have you seen how Sarai's been treating me? Surely you don't expect me to put up with her, do you? She's hard to get along with and impossible to work for!"

The angel says, "If you will go back and submit to her authority, I will bless you by multiplying your descendants."

How did Hagar submit to the Lord? By following the angel's instructions and submitting herself to Sarai. When Hagar submitted to Sarai, she also submitted to the Lord. If she had not submitted, she would have rebelled against God. We submit to the Lord by submitting to authorities on earth, no matter how harshly they may treat us.

> **Humility and submission go together, just as pride and rebellion are interlocked.**

Jesus recognized that human authorities were granted those positions from above. Pilate told Jesus, "Do you not know that I have authority to release you, and I have authority to crucify you?" Jesus answered, "You would have no authority over Me, unless it had been given you from above" (John 19:10–11). Jesus looked past the arrogance of an earthly ruler and saw His Father permitting Pilate's authority.

Principle #3: Submission Requires a Heart of Humility

Humility and submission go together, just as pride and rebellion are interlocked. "Therefore humble yourselves under the mighty hand of God, that He may exalt you at the proper time" (1 Peter 5:6).

The only one who can submit yourself is yourself, and the only one who can humble yourself is the same guy—*yourself*. To submit yourself, you must first humble yourself. Sometimes an authority will tell you to do something that you do not like. The only way that you can submit is through having a humble heart, willing to lay down your rights.

Because humility and submission are linked together, submission is impossible without humility, which is a heart that bows and completely surrenders to God.

Principle #4: Submission to Authority Results in Joyful Obedience

Submission and obedience are not the same. Submission is an inner attitude while obedience is an outward action. Submission is an attitude that results in joyful obedience. If you obey with a grudging attitude, you are not submitting.

A little boy disobeyed his mom, so she ordered him to go sit in the corner. After he went to the corner, he said, "I am sitting down on the outside, but I am standing up on the inside!" He obeyed but he did not submit.

God wants us to submit and obey, even when we might not totally agree with what the authority tells us to do. We should obey with a good attitude because the Lord is the one who told us to do it, and we want to be pleasing to Him.

> **Submission is an inner attitude while obedience is an outward action.**

Authority is usually expressed in words. A policeman just has to say "stop" and you will stop. He says, "Give me your driver's license," and you will give him your license. He might be thirty years younger than you, but he can do that because he is under the police chief, who is under the authority of the city. You will submit to the police officer because you recognize his authority.

But suppose the officer is wearing civilian clothes and asks you to give him your driver's license. You will not do it because you *do not* recognize his authority. You will only submit if you acknowledge and respect the position of authority over you.

Those who rebel refuse to yield to the authority in charge. The Lord wants us to respond to those over us with joyful obedience, not grudgingly or with anger.

Principle #5: We Gain Spiritual Authority by Submitting Ourselves

If you want to be over, you have to be under. God will not promote you to be *in* authority until you first learn how to be *under* authority. All authority comes by placing yourself under somebody. If you are a student in a classroom, you are under the authority of your teacher, who is under the authority of the principal, who is under the authority of the superintendent. This chain of command goes back thousands of years.

A Roman centurion officer asked Jesus to heal his slave. Jesus said, "I will come and heal him." The centurion answered, "Lord, I am not worthy for You to come under my roof, but just say the word, and my servant will be healed" (see Matthew 8:5–10).

The centurion did not appeal to Jesus by saying, "I am a man *in* authority." Instead, he said, "I also am a man *under* authority" (emphasis added). The centurion was in submission to the officers over him and ultimately to the emperor.

The centurion could order his soldiers to come and go because he received his authority by submitting to his superiors. All he had to do was speak the order and it would be done. He did not have to twist their arms. Every Roman soldier understood the importance of respecting the chain of command. The centurion's orders carried the same authority as if the emperor himself were speaking.

When the centurion said, "I *too* am a man under authority," he understood that Jesus had also submitted Himself to His Father. Since He was in total submission, the words of Jesus carried the authority of the Father. Jesus could order the slave's infirmity to leave and it would have to obey—just like the soldiers had to leave when the centurion ordered them to go.

Jesus marveled at this centurion's faith. The Greek word *marveled* means "to be astonished." He was astonished to find someone who actually understood that authority comes from submission. Christ turned to His followers and said, "Do you see this Gentile? I want you to learn from him. He has more faith than anyone in Israel because he understands how authority and submission work."

Again, you gain authority through submission. Spiritual authority to resist the devil comes through submitting ourselves to God. James said, "Submit therefore to God. Resist the devil and he will flee from you" (James 4:7). Many people who quote this verse will say, "Resist the devil and he will flee." But they leave off the first part, "submit therefore to God," which is the key to understanding the passage.

Notice the order. First submit to God and then you can resist the devil. Why? Your authority from God comes through submission. If you are yielding to God, He then grants His authority so you can resist the devil. If you have been struggling with temptation and have a hard time resisting the devil, it might be because you have not completely submitted to the lordship of Jesus Christ.

Principle #6: When Authorities Are in Conflict, Submit to the Higher Authority

Are there cases where you should not submit? Yes. If a boss or ruler asks you to do something immoral, unethical, or to disobey God's Word, you are not obligated to submit.

There was an incident in the early Church where the religious leaders told the disciples not to speak in the name of Jesus. Peter and John replied, "Do you think God wants us to obey you rather than him? We cannot stop telling about everything we have seen and heard" (Acts 4:18–20, NLT).

Not long after this, when the high priest told Peter and the apostles to stop teaching about Jesus, they responded, "We must obey God rather than men" (Acts 5:29). They did not get vicious and hateful toward the high priest. Christians need to always be gracious toward unbelievers. Peter said, "We're sorry, but we can't do that."

Instead of angrily rebelling, they chose to humbly submit to the *higher* authority. Whenever we encounter situations in which two or more authorities are in conflict, we should yield to the highest one without despising the lower one.

Let's say you are at your job and the assistant manager tells you to move a display to a certain location. A few minutes later, the manager tells you to move it to a different place. Which one should you obey? You need to obey the manager because he is the higher authority.

I once drove up to an intersection where an accident had occurred. A policeman stood in the intersection directing traffic. Although the traffic light was red, the policeman waved for me to drive through the red light. Which authority should I obey—the traffic light or the policeman?

In that instance, the traffic cop was a higher authority than the traffic light. I submitted to the higher authority. I did not rebel against all traffic lights from then on. I respected both, but I could not obey both at the same time.

You might encounter some situations where authorities are in conflict. Submit to the higher authority. If that person demands that you violate a scriptural principle, you should always submit to what God says.

Five Authorities

No matter where you live, you will always have a person in authority telling you what to do. As you drive on the roads, it is the Highway Patrol. In your neighborhood, it is the city telling you what you can and cannot build. On the job, a supervisor tells you what to do. The government tells you how much you owe in taxes.

God places a very high value on authority and your proper response to it. The secret to a good life is to learn to submit to these five authorities.

1. God

The Kingdom of God is built on the authority of the Lord Jesus Christ. Jesus said, "All authority has been given to Me in heaven and on earth" (Matthew 28:18). A Christian is someone who has received Jesus as the ultimate authority in his or her life and submits to Him.

SECRET #9

Serve God as your main boss in every area.

The word *Lord* as used in the New Testament means "boss" in today's language. We naturally do not want anyone telling us what to do. We want to be the captain of our own ship and make our own decisions about what we will and will not do. The essence of sin is a rebellious heart that wants to do its own thing.

But we cannot sit on the same throne with Jesus, where we both are in charge. Anything with two heads is a monster. God cannot be the boss of our lives as long as we are on top. For Jesus to become the Lord of our lives, our hearts must change. We need to step down from the throne and let Him rule. We must allow the Holy Spirit to convict us so we surrender to His lordship.

When we submit to Him, we will not only obey what He tells us to do, but we will also submit to the human institutions that He has established on earth.

2. Government

Many people do not want to submit to their government because they do not agree with the policies that are funded by their taxes. That is understandable. It is true that politicians will misuse funds and many government programs are wasteful. But let us remember that God is the One who told us to submit to government. He certainly knew that the authorities would make many wrong decisions. As you read the following verses about submitting to government, keep in mind that the readers of that day were living under an extremely corrupt Roman government. The emperors were cruel dictators, who were persecuting Christians for not worshipping them. Yet, here is what the apostle Paul says:

Let everyone be subject to the governing authorities, for there is no authority except that which God has established. The authorities that exist have been established by God. Consequently, whoever rebels against the authority is rebelling against what God has instituted, and those who do so will bring judgment on themselves. For rulers hold no terror for those who do right, but for those who do wrong.

Do you want to be free from fear of the one in authority? Then do what is right, and you will be commended. For the one in authority is God's servant for your good. But if you do wrong, be afraid, for rulers do not bear the sword for no reason. They are God's servants, agents of wrath to bring punishment on the wrongdoer.

Therefore, it is necessary to submit to the authorities, not only because of possible punishment but also as a matter of conscience. This is also why you pay taxes, for the authorities are God's servants, who give their full time to governing.

Romans 13:1–6, NIV

Notice that God establishes governments and that He called them His servants. Without some kind of government, we would have no order in society. The Scriptures are very clear about this and were written under governmental authorities who were anything but Christian. The apostle Peter also confirms this:

> For the sake of the Lord submit yourselves to every human authority: to the Emperor, who is the supreme authority, and to the governors, who have been appointed by him to punish the evildoers and to praise those who do good.
>
> 1 Peter 2:13–14, GNT

Submitting to authority does not mean that you agree with all their policies. You must obey them until you are told to do something against your convictions, such as denying Jesus as Lord. You can still be courteous and willing to pay the consequences. Your refusal to submit will likely cause you to be persecuted.

In the book of Daniel, Shadrach, Meshach and Abednego submitted to King Nebuchadnezzer until he ordered them to bow down to his golden image. They told him, "Let it be known to you, O king, that we are not going to serve your gods or worship the golden image that you have set up" (Daniel 3:18). They refused to bow to anyone or anything but the Most High God.

The Biblical Responses to Government

The Scriptures have already laid out the responses we must have toward government:

Honor the King

You do not honor a person if you speak in a detrimental way about him to others. God tells us to honor the king. First Peter

2:17 says, "Honor all people, love the brotherhood, fear God, honor the king." If you honor the king, you will not make fun of him, no matter how much you may disagree with his policies.

Even though Saul was a wicked king and constantly tried to kill him, David respected Saul's position as ruler and refused to take his life when he had the opportunity. David said, "The LORD forbid that I should stretch out my hand against the LORD's anointed" (1 Samuel 26:11). He had a great respect for authority, which is lacking in many people today.

When Paul stood before Ananias, the high priest ordered him to be struck in the mouth. In response to being hit, Paul said, "God is going to strike you, you whitewashed wall!"

The bystanders said, "Do you revile God's high priest?"

Paul answered, "I was not aware, brethren, that he was high priest, for it is written, 'You shall not speak evil of a ruler of your people'" (see Acts 23:2–5).

Did you catch that insight? The Lord does not want you to speak even one evil word against a ruler, which includes the elected officials over you. Although you may not agree with the views of the politicians, you can be respectful in your disagreement.

Pray for Those in Authority

Christians have a responsibility to pray for those in positions of authority. Paul told us,

> I urge, then, first of all, that petitions, prayers, intercession and thanksgiving be made for all people—for kings and all those in authority, that we may live peaceful and quiet lives in all godliness and holiness. This is good, and pleases God our Savior.
>
> 1 Timothy 2:1–3, NIV

Prayer is precisely what leaders desperately need as the spirit of anarchy seems to be gaining strength by the hour.

While intercession not only helps those in charge to make wise decisions, it also keeps our own hearts in check, since it is unlikely we will detest anyone we are praying for.

Pay Your Taxes

Jesus told us to "render to Caesar the things that are Caesar's" (Mark 12:17). We might not want to pay our taxes to an ungodly government or agree with the way they use our money. Even so, Jesus said we need to pay our taxes. Since Christ is the one who told us to do this, we should view paying taxes as an act of obedience that is pleasing to God, just as we give tithes to please Him. He will reward us in heaven for fulfilling this responsibility to government authorities.

Participate by Voting

Each form of government gives citizens differing ways to participate. In a democracy we have the right to vote. If we do not actively participate in the governmental process, we have no right to complain about who is elected or what they do.

3. Jobs

God wants you to obey that boss you do not like. You have no idea how difficult his job is, and you are making it harder when you gripe and complain. Perhaps it is for this reason that Peter says, "Servants, be submissive to your masters with all respect, not only to those who are good and gentle, but *also to those who are unreasonable*" (1 Peter 2:18, emphasis added). Paul adds, "Urge bondslaves to be subject to their own masters in everything, to be well-pleasing, not argumentative" (Titus 2:9).

Do you think Paul and Peter knew every master in the world? Of course not. They did not say, "You can submit to a good master, but you do not have to submit to the one that is a jerk!" Instead, they gave the same instruction to everyone who read their letters—submit to every master, whether they are good or unreasonable.

Employees must follow the same instructions that were given to slaves toward their masters.

> Slaves, obey your earthly masters with respect and fear, and with sincerity of heart, just as you would obey Christ. Obey them not only to win their favor when their eye is on you, but as slaves of Christ, doing the will of God from your heart. Serve wholeheartedly, as if you were serving the Lord, not people.
>
> Ephesians 6:5–7, NIV

Although you may not agree with your boss, God wants you to cheerfully submit to him or her as if you were serving the Lord: "Whatever you do, do your work heartily, as for the Lord rather than for men. . . . It is the Lord Christ whom you serve" (Colossians 3:23–24).

4. Church

It is nearly impossible to find a church where everyone is in agreement on every issue. To keep ministry flowing smoothly, its members must overrule their own preferences through submission, so that the greater good can be accomplished.

Always remember that "authority" does not mean "superiority" in any way. It simply denotes order. In the Church, God has appointed authorities with the responsibility to lead the flock. To make this work, church members should willingly submit to them. Think of submission as cooperation.

Submission works from the bottom up, not from the top down. No pastor or elder can make anyone submit. If you are going to submit, it has to be *your* idea. It is initiated internally, not externally, and works from the bottom of the hierarchy up, not the top down.

When this godly way of thinking is birthed inside a person's spirit, submitting becomes as natural as breathing. When people submit to their authorities, it empowers them to joyfully carry out their ministries. But when people resist, it is rebellion against God.

Some people will justify their rebellion by disguising it as boldness. I know about a woman who wanted to serve in her church but she did not want to obey her leaders. She helped with the children's ministry but would not cooperate with any of the other workers, which caused conflicts.

To justify her rebellious attitude, she defiantly said, "I only take my orders from God, not from any person! I will not bow down to anyone!"

She overlooked the fact, however, that God has already told us in His Word to submit to those in authority and obey our leaders. When we submit to our church leaders, we *are* submitting to the Lord. Some people never realize that having a respectful attitude toward those in charge is more important to God than the petty issues that concern them.

> Submission works from the bottom up, not from the top down. If you are going to submit, it has to be your idea.

"Obey your leaders and submit to them, for they keep watch over your souls as those who will give an account. Let them do this with joy and not with grief, for this would be unprofitable for you" (Hebrews 13:17). Leaders will find joy when people submit to them, but are filled with grief when people resist and rebel against their leadership.

If you cannot agree with the church leadership, you have the freedom to leave that fellowship without causing a ruckus. It is certainly not wrong to change churches, and it is not being rebellious to leave a place of worship if the pastoral leadership is morally corrupt or doctrinally unsound. Once you settle in a new congregation of your choosing, however, you must humbly submit yourself to the authorities in that place.

> But we request of you, brethren, that you appreciate those who diligently labor among you, and have charge over you in the Lord and give you instruction, and that you esteem them very highly in love because of their work. Live in peace with one another.
>
> 1 Thessalonians 5:12–13

Think how much good churches could accomplish if every member had this attitude.

5. Family

Family is the basic unit of society. Paul begins his instructions on husband and wife relationships by saying, "Be subject to one another in the fear of Christ" (Ephesians 5:21). He tells the wives to be subject to their own husbands as to the Lord, and the husbands must love their wives as Christ loved the Church and gave Himself up for her (see Ephesians 5:23–25).

The husband is the designated leader in the home with the wife as his covenant partner. When the husband loves his wife as Christ loves, it will bring harmony into the home. A man is foolish if he does not allow his wife to be his helper in the leadership role.

Again, this hierarchy has nothing to do with superiority but is talking about establishing order in the home. When it comes to decision-making, the husband has one vote and the wife has one vote. Hopefully husbands and wives will prayerfully make decisions together in agreement. If they are deadlocked on a decision, however, the husband's vote counts a little more as the tiebreaker, and he will give an account to God for it.

God also gives instructions to children:

> Children, obey your parents in the Lord, for this is right. Honor your father and mother (which is the first commandment with a promise), so that it may be well with you, and that you may live long on the earth.
>
> Ephesians 6:1–3

The Lord makes a promise to children who will obey their parents. "That it may be well with you" refers to the *quality* of life. The Lord will make sure things go well for them. "That you may live long on the earth" refers to the *longevity* of life. Both the quality and longevity of life are influenced by a child's obedience. Apparently the Lord keeps track of everyone and the blessing or lack thereof can be traced back to how people responded to their parents as children.

You will remember when Joseph and Mary found Jesus teaching in the temple when He was twelve years old, He said, "Did you not know that I must be about My Father's business?" (Luke 2:49, NKJV). His Father's business did not just involve teaching God's Word, but also submitting to His parents. Jesus went home with them and "continued in subjection to them" (Luke 2:51). He submitted to His parents as an example for us.

Parents need to teach their kids the importance of respecting and obeying authority and the promises that God makes for doing so. When children respect authority at a young age, it is more likely they will also do it as adults. Children are to be submissive to their parents when they live at home, and are to always honor them after they leave.

One final thought. What if you do not like the government, cannot stand your job and disagree with the decisions your church makes? You can always move to another country, find another job and join another church.

But guess what. You will find authorities you will disagree with there, too.

Discussion Questions

To Submit or Not to Submit

Why did God establish authorities on earth?

What should be our motive for submitting to those in authority?

Why is humility an essential attitude in being able to submit?

How can we respect and honor our elected officials, even though we have voted for someone else?

Read Acts 4:18–20 and 5:28–29. What are some situations where we are permitted to disobey the earthly authority in order to submit to the higher authority, God?

Read 1 Peter 2:18. How can your conscience toward God help you joyfully submit to an unreasonable boss?

In what ways can we submit to the authority of our church leaders?

PREPARING FOR DEATH

Every man must do two things alone; he must do his own believing and his own dying.

—Martin Luther

Death is the last but certainly not the least challenge you will face. If you make the right decisions about it, you will prepare for a much better tomorrow—in the next life.

Experiences, especially our first ones, can have an effect on us for either good or bad. Death was never talked about in our home. I never remember going to a funeral or a cemetery. Although my mother had lost four children at birth or shortly after birth, it was never mentioned. I only found out about my predeceased siblings years later.

At the age of fourteen, I had my first experience with death when a classmate drowned in the pool we were swimming in. I still remember seeing his limp body lying on the side of the pool. Even though years have passed since this incident, I have never gotten over it. Perhaps it is for this reason that conducting funerals has always been difficult for me as a minister.

My first funeral was in Cedar Key, Florida, which was a small fishing village. I had no idea what to do, so I borrowed one of the liturgy books from a fellow minister and headed out with my wife as a companion. The service was conducted outside between two local business buildings. The cemetery was so far out in the woods that a guide had to remove fallen trees to get us there. My car had a flat tire on the way, and so my wife and I rode in the hearse.

For my second funeral, the family requested that I only read the twenty-third Psalm; I knew I could do that. That sums up my first experiences with death. Although I have conducted many funerals in my sixty years of ministry since then, it has never been easy for me to do. To this day, it is hard for me to look at someone lying in a casket, primarily because of my childhood experiences.

The Death of Loved Ones

We need to prepare ourselves for the inevitable death of our friends and loved ones, some of which will come before our own demise. My parents died in their eighties, but my brother died in an airplane accident in his early thirties. His death came unexpectedly and was a shock to our entire family. One of my favorite cousins, a doctor, died in his late thirties. We do not expect people to die at such an age, and it is much harder on us when someone dies "before their time."

Although we think everyone deserves to live seventy or eighty years, God never guaranteed such a thing. In fact, no one is even guaranteed tomorrow.

Come now, you who say, "Today or tomorrow we will go to such and such a city, and spend a year there and engage in business and make a profit." Yet you do not know what your life will be like tomorrow. You are just a vapor that appears for a little while and then vanishes away. Instead, you ought to say, "If the Lord wills, we will live and also do this or that."

James 4:13–15

Since no one knows how much time they have left, it is that much more urgent to be prepared for death. Everyone has an appointment with the coffin. "It is appointed for men to die once and after this comes judgment" (Hebrews 9:27). Once that last breath is taken, your spirit will depart from your body and you will enter eternity, in one place or another.

What Is Death?

Death does not mean ceasing to exist, but it is a separation and the inability to relate. Dead eyes cannot relate to light; dead ears cannot relate to sound. A dead body cannot respond to those around it.

Physical death occurs when your spirit separates from your body. James 2:26 says, "The body without the spirit is dead." When you breathe your last, your spirit will depart from your body for its eternal destination.

> **Everyone has an appointment with the coffin.**

A person who is spiritually dead is unable to relate to God. Spiritual death is when a person is spiritually separated from the Lord. If a person dies in this condition, that individual will be cut off from God forever, which is called "the second death" (see Revelation 20:14–15). If that person receives Christ as Lord and Savior, however, he or she will pass from spiritual death into eternal life.

A marriage dies when a husband and wife separate. Nothing is more painful in human relationships than the death of a marriage. The "death of a vision" is a loss of hope. You had a vision for the future, and for one reason or another it did not come to pass. My own death of a vision came when I was about fifty. I had a vision of what a church could be like for the glory of God. A day came when I realized that it was not going to happen. I now have a renewed vision of what I am to do with the rest of my life and I am enjoying every minute.

Preparing for Your Own Death

It may make you feel uncomfortable to think about your own death, but you need to prepare for it in four areas: legally, relationally, practically and spiritually.

1. Legal Preparation

We live in a nation of laws and lawyers, and your death has legal consequences. You can save your loved ones from a lot of frustration by properly preparing a will. It will help them to navigate through the legal proceedings the law requires. You will be able to designate how you want your assets distributed after you are gone. If you do not do this, the court may decide these things, which could create problems for those you leave behind.

You also need to decide whether you would like to donate your eyes, heart, kidneys and other organs to help those who have a physical disability. You cannot do this after you die, so you must decide before then. My wife and I have decided to give our bodies to medical science at the local medical school. We want to go down swinging and doing all we can to help humanity.

You will also need to make preparations for your funeral. Many wise people make their own arrangements, including buying their own cemetery plots. They might also decide how they want their memorial service to be conducted, including their favorite Scriptures and the songs they want sung. This makes it as easy as possible for those who have to take care of those arrangements.

I know this may sound strange, but I have often thought about planning a funeral service that would be somewhat out of the ordinary. I would have one hand sticking out of the casket with a sign saying, "I took nothing with me." I would have the hearse drive around town with a sign that reads, "You may be next."

If I could write something on my tombstone, I would have a Scripture that summed up what I wanted my life to be. A headstone will usually have the person's name, date of birth and date of death with a period after it. It typically reads something like this:

John Smith. 1956–1999.
The period means "the end."

But I would have my gravestone written like this:
Peter Lord. 1929–2020,—

I would have a comma because my physical death is not the end of me, followed by a long line indicating that eternity is forever. I would do all this to remind people that we are just passing through this planet and everyone needs to get ready for the next world.

2. Practical Preparation

Three days before comedian Bob Hope died, his daughter asked him where he wanted to be buried. He told her, "Surprise me." Hope lived to be one hundred years old but had not taken the time to pick out a cemetery plot before he passed away. He failed to practically prepare for his death. Some people prepare for their funeral in unusual ways. Frederic Baur invented the method of uniformly stacking potato chips inside a Pringles can instead of a bag. When he died in 2008, his children stopped at Walgreens on the way to the funeral home and bought a can of Pringles. Baur was cremated and his ashes were placed inside the Pringles can for burial.

In the event I die before my wife, I do not want to be surprised like Bob Hope or buried in a can like Fred Baur, so I have written down detailed instructions for her. I have included the names and phone numbers of the best service people that she will need, and details about where the important papers are located, such as titles to the house and car. I have also written down all the information for our banks and insurance companies, and who she will need to contact regarding Social Security benefits. I have tried to think through everything she and the children will need so that the affairs can be wrapped up as easily as possible.

I cannot tell you how many times people have told me that the loved one who passed away did not leave any of the above information, and this caused them great difficulty. You can at least be thoughtful to those who will have the responsibility of taking care of your business. By leaving the appropriate information, it will be a tremendous help to those who are left behind, especially if you have handled those responsibilities and no one else knows whom to contact. Write the important things down, and do it today.

3. Relational Preparation

Sooner or later you will find out that nothing in life is more important than relationships. Due to our sinfulness, it is not uncommon to experience conflict and hurt feelings. God wants you to do all that you can to resolve your issues, especially with family and close friends. The best thing you can do right now is to make sure you get things right with people before you pass away. You do not want to die without telling people that you love them, that you forgive them or that you ask their forgiveness. Closure is good for you and them.

> **Make sure you get things right with people before you pass away.**

Make sure your relationships are up to date. You might need to get on the phone and call someone that you have not talked with in years. Seek to be reconciled, ask forgiveness when it is necessary, pay all the debts you owe and express gratitude to all who have helped you in life's journey.

4. Spiritual Preparation

People have one of two views on death and the afterlife. One view is that when a person dies, it is the end of his or her existence. Life is over. Finished. Done. And they hope they are right.

The other view is that when a person dies, it is a transition of a person's existence into another world. The physical body stops living, but the inner person, the spirit, either goes to heaven or hell. The Scriptures teach that Christians do not have to grieve at the death of a believer, while unbelievers grieve because they do not have any hope of the afterlife (see 1 Thessalonians 4:13).

One day your name will be chiseled on a headstone. You will be laid to rest in a casket, lowered into the ground, and then everyone will go back to the church and eat potato salad.

But your spirit will go into eternity where you will exist forever. That can be a scary thought, depending on your relationship with God.

The Other Side of Death's Door

Everyone wants to know what happens after we die. When Jesus rose from the dead, He answered that question and took the mystery out of death. We do not have to speculate anymore about which religion is right. We do not have to wonder what lies beyond the grave, or how to get to heaven. Jesus told us what is on the other side of the grave.

Imagine watching people go through a door into a building, but no one ever comes back out through that door. Every day hundreds of people go in but not a single person returns. This goes on for years. How would you know what is on the other side of the door?

Some people try to guess what is on the other side. They form an opinion and try to convince others to believe just like them. If they can fool enough people, they can start their own religion. The more people that follow their assumption, the more popular their religion will be. And this is how the world's religions got started.

The foundation for these religions, however, is based on speculation and is therefore not reliable. The only way you can know what is on the other side is if a trustworthy person goes through the door, and then does what no one else can do—returns through it.

Jesus took the mystery out of what lies beyond the grave by going through death's door and coming back to life three days later. That is the difference between Jesus and the religions of the world. The other religions are just speculating, but Jesus proved He is the Truth by rising from the dead. He revealed that there are only two destinations on the other side of the grave—heaven and hell. You are betting your soul on whether or not you believe His words.

SECRET #10

Receive Jesus Christ as your Lord and you will never have to fear death.

God does not want anyone to go to hell but for everyone to come to repentance (see 2 Peter 3:9). Hell is a place for all who reject Jesus Christ and His sacrifice for their sins. When Christ died on the cross, He paid for the sins of the world, including yours. When you call out to Him by faith and surrender your life to Him, He will forgive your sins and give you eternal life. When you die, your spirit will leave your body and will go to be with Him in heaven.

To receive Jesus Christ as your Lord and Savior, pray this with a sincere heart:

Heavenly Father, I realize that I am a sinner and need to be saved. Lord Jesus, thank You for becoming my sacrifice for sin by dying on the cross. I ask You to come into my life and save me. I give You my life, and I will follow You the rest of my days. Take me to heaven when I die. Thank You for saving me! Amen.

If you sincerely prayed that prayer, you are now a Christian. Because you now have eternal life, you do not need to be afraid of dying. You can tell Him, "Lord, You told me that I do not have to be afraid of death and I trust Your promise."

No Fear in Death

People are afraid to die because they do not know where they are going in the afterlife. Now that you have received

Jesus Christ into your life as Lord and Savior, you have no reason to fear death. Jesus came that He "might free those who through fear of death were subject to slavery all their lives" (Hebrews 2:15). That means you do not need to be afraid of dying. Dying is the last thing that you are going to do on earth, and Jesus does not want you to be miserable or tormented by worrying about it. He came to set you free so that you can enjoy life, not fear death.

A family was riding in their car when a bee flew in the open window. The girl in the car was allergic to bees and if she got stung, she could die. When the father caught the bee with his hand, his daughter relaxed. Then the dad opened his hand and the bee started flying around again.

When the little girl started to panic again, her father said, "You do not need to be afraid anymore. The bee only has one stinger, and it stung me in the hand. Now it cannot hurt you because its stinger is gone."

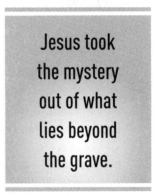

Jesus took the mystery out of what lies beyond the grave.

When Jesus rose from the dead, He removed the sting of death for those who believe in Him. The Scripture says, "O death, where is your victory? O death, where is your sting?" (1 Corinthians 15:55). Just like a bee loses its stinger when it stings someone, death lost its sting when it stung Jesus. For those who love Him, there will be no pain at all in death.

So what is death like for a Christian? The Bible describes it as sleeping. It does not hurt to fall asleep, does it? Death is not to be dreaded either because Jesus took the fear out of death.

A little boy asked his mother, "Mom, what is it like to die?"

She told her son, "Do you remember when you fell asleep in the living room, and your father picked you up in his arms and put you in your bed? You fell asleep in one room and woke up in another room. That is what death is like for a believer in Christ. You fall asleep in one room and wake up in another room. You will fall asleep on earth and wake up in heaven."

Not only do you not have to fear death, you also do not need to be afraid of losing your eternal life. "Eternal" means never-ending. Jesus made this promise to His children: "I give eternal life to them, and they will never perish; and no one will snatch them out of My hand" (John 10:28). Trust in His promise and it will remove your fear.

Preparing for Your Future Home

Two caterpillars were crawling across a hot sidewalk when a beautiful butterfly flew over them. One caterpillar looked up and said, "I wouldn't get up in that thing for a million dollars!"

Death is not the end but a transition into a better life that will never end. It is hard for us to grasp that heaven is a far better place than here. It is also difficult for us to grasp that all believers will be transformed from caterpillar status to butterfly status when we receive our resurrection bodies.

You have already taken your first step in preparing for physical death by receiving Jesus Christ as your Lord. But you now have an opportunity to prepare for a better tomorrow in the next world. Jesus said to "lay up for yourselves treasures in heaven" (Matthew 6:20, NKJV). I have already discussed this in the chapter about handling your money, but I would like to reinforce this important instruction.

Accepting Christ into your life determines your eternal *destination*—heaven. How you live after you are saved until the time you die determines your eternal *occupation*—what you will be doing in heaven. You will be rewarded for your faithfulness in serving Christ during your remaining time on this planet. Your rewards will be privileges in the next life. We do not know what they are, although they will be beyond our wildest imaginations.

Here are some of the things that God says He will reward forever:

- Being martyred for Christ (see Hebrews 11:37)
- Being persecuted for His name's sake (see Luke 6:22–23)
- Suffering for the Lord (see Mark 10:37–39)
- Leading someone to salvation (see Proverbs 11:30; Luke 16:9)
- Cheerfully giving your money in offerings (see Matthew 6:3–4, 19–20)
- Diligently seeking God (see Hebrews 11:6)
- Helping those who cannot repay you (see Luke 14:12–14)
- Telling the message of salvation to someone (see 1 Corinthians 9:16–17)
- Praying (see Matthew 6:6)
- Fasting (see Matthew 6:17–18)
- Being a good steward of your money (see Luke 16:11–12)
- Faithfully serving the Lord (see Luke 19:17; 1 Corinthians 15:58)
- Lending to others without expecting anything back (see Luke 6:35)
- Loving your enemies (see Luke 6:35; Matthew 5:46)
- Doing good deeds (see Ephesians 6:7–8)
- Doing little things for others such as giving a cup of water (see Matthew 10:42)

- Financially supporting those who serve in ministry (see Matthew 10:41)
- Working faithfully at your job (see Colossians 3:22–24)
- Submitting with respect to unreasonable employers (see 1 Peter 2:18–20)
- Having a servant's attitude (see Mark 10:43–45)
- Humbling yourself (see Matthew 18:4; Luke 14:11)
- Helping the poor (see Proverbs 19:17)
- Visiting widows and orphans in their distress (see James 1:27)
- Living righteously (see Proverbs 11:31)
- Persevering under trials and temptations (see James 1:12)

If you are doing the things mentioned above, you are laying up treasures for yourself in heaven, which is wisely preparing for the afterlife. You will not see your rewards until after you die, but you will not be disappointed. "He who believes in Him *will not be disappointed*" (1 Peter 2:6, emphasis added).

I look forward to meeting you one day. Probably not here, but in the next world!

Discussion Questions

From the Womb to the Tomb and Beyond

To prepare for death, take a trip to a cemetery and read the ages on the headstones. Think about how long they lived and how long they have been in eternity. How does this affect the way you view your own life?

Read what was written on the tombstones by their loved ones. What will people say about your life after you have passed on?

As you sit on a bench in the cemetery, ask yourself what decisions you will be glad that you made when it is your time to be buried.

In what ways have you prepared practically and legally for your own death?

How can you "get right" with people before you die?

Carefully examine the list of items that God will reward. How many of those things are you currently doing? Which of those things will you start doing today?

A FINAL WORD

Now you know how to overcome the ten greatest challenges that you will face in life. Remember, you are the player on the field and only you can fulfill your role in the game of life. Make a decision right now that you are going to win. Read your "playbook," the Bible, every day. As you pray, listen for the "Head Coach" to whisper further instructions. The Lord will always show you what to do when you ask for wisdom.

I pray that you will take action in addressing the challenges that you will encounter. Your main obstacle is not a lack of information but a lack of *application*. "Therefore, to one who knows the right thing to do and does not do it, to him it is sin" (James 4:17). As you apply the biblical principles set forth in this book, the Lord will bring victory in your life for obeying Him.

At the end of your game, I will be waiting to meet you in the locker room. Together, we will celebrate your victory—for all of eternity!

Peter Lord was born in Kingston, Jamaica. Raised on a cattle ranch and banana plantation, he moved to the United States in 1946 for a college education. He graduated in 1950 and the next year married Johnnie Sapp. Peter and Johnnie pastored two small churches in Florida before he began seminary in 1954. After graduating in 1957, he pastored three churches in Florida, the last for thirty years—Park Avenue Baptist Church in Titusville, at the north gate of Cape Kennedy and the space center complex.

The father of five children—which he declares to be the best practical education he has received in real-life living—Peter traveled across the United States for ten years after retiring, ministering in about 250 churches of all kinds and sizes. In recent years God has called him to disciple some people at his home in Titusville. Peter's oldest son is now the pastor of Park Avenue Baptist Church, and one of his nine grandchildren serves on the staff.

Peter's major goals include enabling people to be conscious of God in everyday life and to finish life with the thrill of victory. The theme of his ministry is *to keep the main thing the main thing* and to encourage others to do the same. He gives credit to the everlasting tender mercies of Abba Father for anything he is, for anything he might have done to aid in glorifying Christ and for any part he has played in building the Kingdom of God.

Kent Crockett graduated from Texas A&M University and Southwestern Baptist Theological Seminary. He is discipleship pastor at Journey Church in Prattville, Alabama, and is the author of *The 911 Handbook, Making Today Count for Eternity* and *I Once Was Blind but Now I Squint.* Kent and his wife, Cindy, have two children. His website is www.kentcrockett.com.

More From Peter Lord

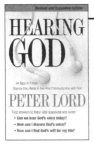

Christians often struggle with prayer because it has become a one-way conversation with the ceiling. It doesn't have to be this way! In this updated edition of the classic bestseller *Hearing God*, Peter Lord offers a step-by-step guide to developing a rich prayer life—moving you from one-way communication *to* God to two-way communication *with* God.

Hearing God

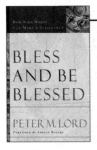

In our negative world, the power of positive words shines brightly. *Bless and Be Blessed* shows you how to weave the practice of affirming others into your daily life—an action that will have a positive impact on yourself and those around you. With scriptural basis, spiritual insight and personal stories, Peter Lord teaches you how to bless and be blessed in return.

Bless and Be Blessed

Chosen
chosenbooks.com